SERVING GOD'S PURPOSE
IN OUR GENERATION

Bill Beckworth

ISAIAH 55 PUBLISHING
P.O. Box 1147
Decatur, GA 30032

Edited by Russell Holt
Cover design by Robert Nigel Mason
Interior design by Ariel Fuentealba
Typeset in 11/13 New Century Schoolbook

All Scripture references not otherwise credited are from the New
King James Version.

99 00 01 02 03 • 5 4 3 2 1

Dedication

*Dedicated to my wife and sweetheart
Connie, who has been a great source of
encouragement in our special ministry
not only to me but to 100's of Literature
Evangelists and publishing leaders
through the years.*

Comments from those who read the manuscript

Serving God's Purpose in Our Generation *is a book that will be of great value to seasoned Literature Evangelists as well as those just starting this work—or contemplating doing so. I read the book in manuscript form and found it to be quite well written. I especially appreciated the fact that the author has included a number of personal stories illustrating the points he is making. These make the book entertaining as well as informative.* Serving God's Purpose in Our Generation *is filled with practical advice, inspiring stories, and valuable tips on how to be successful in the Literature Ministry. It would be particularly helpful to English-speaking persons around the world who are engaged in this work.*

Russell Holt
Vice President/Product Development
Pacific Press

The author of this book is a personal friend and career publishing leader. Bill has served in North America and Africa in the nearly 30 years he has given to Literature Evangelism. His wide experience in working with different cultures, including trips to eastern Europe and Russia makes him well qualified to author this book. I trust that as you read you will be blessed and become a better worker for Jesus.

Ron Appenzeller
Publishing Director
General Conference

The book, Serving God's Purpose in our Generation, *by Elder Bill Beckworth, the long time and much experienced leader and Publishing Director for the Southern Union in the North American Division is a much needed publication for inspiration and training for Literature Evangelists. It is deserving of wide sales and circulation.*

I highly recommend it to North America and the other divisions of the world field.

Robert S. Smith
Publishing Director
North American Division

I was pleased to read the interesting and inspiring message written by Bill Beckworth. His practical counsel for Christian selling and depending on God's leadership are sure to be a blessing to those interested in Literature Ministry or for the active Literature Evangelist professional. I urge you to consider using this timely book in recruiting and strengthening a Literature workforce in the future.

Bob Kyte
President
Pacific Press

I recently read your manuscript, submitted to Pacific Press. I read it with great interest. It was very well written.

The information that you have gathered from your years of experience and put in written form, will, in my mind, be of great interest to all Literature Evangelists in their selling program.

Publishing Directors and Associates will greatly benefit in the use of the material in your book as added material for their training schools. I plan to use it in future training schools in our territory.

Felix Castro
Director
Subscription Sales
Pacific Press & HHES

Table of Contents

"For when David had served God's purpose in his own generation, he fell asleep..."

—Acts 13:36, NIV

Introduction

Why this book? Originally, my motive in producing this book was to provide an instructional manual for literature evangelists that was relevant, practical, and interesting. As you will discover, however, an additional theme was developed within this book: literature evangelism's role in God's last day work. No other denomination has a ministry like it. The history of the Seventh-day Adventist Church cannot be told without relating the story of the publishing work.

J. N. Andrews, as the church's first missionary, established a publishing work to further the Adventist message in Europe. The same story could be told of most places where our work has been established. If not a printing press, it was a literature evangelist and his selling of books that brought the Seventh-day Adventist message to new areas. An estimated 80 percent of new fields were first opened by literature evangelists.

The printing and selling of the three angels' message has never been easy. The church fathers sacrificed much in establishing the publishing work. Ellen White had three visions about publishing before James and the brethren became serious about it. The first two chapters of Publishing Ministry are full of the sacrificial struggles encountered in launching the publishing work. Yet, in spite of these challenges, God promised success: "After coming out of vision I said to my husband '...It will be a success from the first. From this small beginning it was shown to be like streams of light that went clear around the world." C.M. p. 1.

In 1861, the church was organized. For what reason? To have a church that would be the legal property holder of the publishing work. The publishing work existed several years before our church even had a name. The relation of the Christian church to business has been a point of contention throughout history, and this is also true of the publishing work in our church. Some factions believe that the church should not be involved in any business. This argument fails to acknowledge the reality that the church is a big business. The publishing work is both business and ministry. This work was established and has continued because of inspired counsel.

George King, a Canadian, contributed to the development of the publishing work with his selling of Adventist magazine subscriptions to the public. In 1880, King and J. H. Wilcox began selling a 1,600 page health book by J. H. Kellogg. In 1882, he sold Daniel and Revelation *by Uriah Smith. This added a great driving force to the church's outreach. Our literature evangelists and books began to reach many unentered areas. George King gave the rest of his life to the literature ministry. Today there are approximately 25,000 literature evangelists in the world field.*

God has blessed the publishing work. He continues to do so as He works with each literature evangelist. Therefore, the two themes of this book, the mechanics and rationale of literature evangelism, are presented in the hope that God may use them so literature evangelists and the literature ministry may continue to serve and glorify God. If this book will help anyone become more effective or stay by the calling, I will give all praises to Him that is worthy! This church and this ministry has given my life real purpose and direction. I am just thankful to be a part of His last day work.

Chapter 1

*"But the seed on good soil stands for those with
a noble and good heart, who hear the word,
retain it, and by persevering produce a crop."*
Luke 8:15, NIV

Thank You, Bookmen

Most church members can point with enthusiasm to individuals whom God used in their conversion. And most, though unaware of it, were influenced by tracts or books. Many years ago Ellen White rightly said, "The publishing branch of our cause has much to do with our power." C.M., p. 148. The reformer Martin Luther said of the press, "A drop of ink will make a million think."

Long ago when farmers in Kansas still farmed with horses, a colporteur, now more often called a literature evangelist, walked across the windswept plains of Kansas calling on the small farming communities and selling his truth-filled books. He stopped a man who was plowing with a team of horses in his field and canvassed him. The farmer was interested and invited him home. The farmer, Mr Henry V. Chinn, and his wife Francis not only bought his book, but accepted the message in the book. The Chinns and other individuals in the small farming town of Latham, Kansas, just a few miles east of Wichita, Kansas joined the Seventh-day Adventist Church. This dedicated worker's name is unknown today except in heaven, but his legacy continues. According to the eye witnesses who have now passed away, he carried his books in a carpet bag. He must have been very dedicated and sincerely

believed in his mission. He must have left his home and family
for extended periods of time on his important mission trips. It
could be said of him like David of old that he "served God's purpose in his generation."

When I met the Chinns in 1965, Francis was in her mid 70's
and Henry was 80. I had just moved to Wichita from a small
town and was beginning my junior year at Wichita State University. I was also just hired to work the evening shift at Boeing
Aircraft. I was moving there from the small town of Coffeyville,
Kansas, 150 miles away. My hope was to find a place where I
could rent a room and get meals. My time was very limited. Provi-
dentially, a friend in Coffeyville told me he knew of such a place.
He once stayed there and recommended the lady's food. It was the
Chinn family. God was leading, although I was not yet aware of it.

Following my friend's suggestion I found the Chinn's home
and never looked for another. Mrs. Chinn did cook good food. She
was past the age where most people work full time but she worked
harder than most young people. Mr. Chinn was getting a little
senile but he could remember all the famous Adventist "proof
texts" which I tried to ignore. The thing that impressed me most
was the kind and cheerful spirit of this hard working, elderly
woman.

I could only remember hearing of a Seventh-day Adventist
once when I was nine. My father came home one evening telling
of a man who would leave work one hour before sundown on Friday because it was the beginning of his Sabbath. My father, who
claimed to be agnostic on occasions, only saw it as humorous. I
remember going to a calendar and counting the days and telling
my parents, "Well, Saturday is the seventh day." Now 14 years
later I was confronted with the Sabbath again along with the
most positive testimony for Christ and this message—a kind and
cheerful witness.

I tried to avoid the witness of the Chinns. I didn't want it to
affect me, but it did more than I knew. My church membership
was in the Southern Baptist Convention, and I sometimes
attended the Methodist Church. Occasionally when the Chinn's
were able to persuade me to join them for a short Bible study, I
would leave saying to myself, "They were right again." Also during the two years I had stayed with the them, Mrs. Chinn was
like a mother to me, and whenever possible she would give me
something to read.

Occasionally, I read some of it when I could find time in my busy schedule. Two years later, I married my college sweetheart, Connie. We lived a few miles from the Chinns, and they did not lose contact with us.

Connie and I had been married six months when a small reaping series was held by Elder Bill Hatch, Central Union Conference Home Missionary Leader. Mrs. Chinn had us over for lunch and called three different times before she got us to attend our first meeting. Finally we attended out of courtesy to her, not necessarily seekers, but the Lord convicted Connie and me. We were attending a Baptist church that boasted a membership of 3,000 but we joined a little Adventist Church on Dodge Street with about 250 active members. We had caught a vision, not of a church on Dodge Street but of a world-wide movement that was taking a message to every tongue, tribe and people.

I will be eternally grateful to the Chinn family for their faithful and persistent witness, even when it appeared to them that they were not reaching me. I look forward to the resurrection morning when I shall greet them. I will also be looking for Elder Brewer, our local pastor who has passed away. He took a special interest in us and continued Bible studies with us after we joined the church. I give thanks also for the vision and energy of Elder Hatch who left his administrative duties to hold that effort. You know someone else I want to meet on that great day? You guessed it—that colporteur who walked across those plains with a carpetbag selling books. He changed the Chinn's lives for this earth and eternity. Think of the contribution that family made through the years! Think of the tithe they paid; the ministers that tithe supported; the missions they always contributed to faithfully. They won others to the church in addition to Connie and me. I am so grateful for that colporteur's vision and sacrifice. He was away from his family and home for weeks and maybe months, but influenced more people for eternity than he could probably imagine. Connie and I have had the privilege of working in the literature ministry for three decades.

The literature evangelist ministry is unique to our church. At any time of day, someone somewhere on this planet is selling our books. As we draw closer to the end of time, God is calling special individuals to enter this important work full time. There is no other ministry in our church where one person can reach so many people with the gospel in such a permanent and powerful way as with the printed page. On every continent literature evangelist are writing a modern Book of Acts. I want to say a big Thank You to these mighty men and women of the cross both of yesteryear and today. I personally owe you so much and so do so many in our church. It will be said of them as of King David, "They served God's purpose in their generation."

Chapter 2

"So shall my word be that goeth forth out of my mouth; it shall not return unto me void, but it shall accomplish that which I please, and it shall prosper in the thing whereto I sent it." Isaiah 55:11, KJV.

Jesus Our Example

Jesus is our example in everything, including salesmanship! Once I was discussing selling our literature with a minister. He told me, "I couldn't sell our books because that is manipulating people." My response was, "When you preach a sermon, do you have an introduction that warms the people up? Do you have a body to your thoughts? Do you try to give the congregation a conviction to do the Lord's will and create in them a desire to follow the Lord? Do you then call the people to some kind of action at the close of your sermon? Do you ask for a decision? If you do these things, then you have made a great sales presentation." Because that's what it takes whether you're selling our books, cars, real estate, stocks and bonds or preaching a sermon. A well-written article also has these steps. Selling has a bad implication to some people simply because they do not understand.

The irate lady said in a demeaning tone, "I wrote on that card I mailed to your company for them not to send a salesman." The literature evangelist looked back at the lady, smiled and said, "Well ma'am, they sent me, and I'm the poorest example of a salesman they have!" As he chuckled, she smiled, relaxed and said, "Come in." The truth is that he was really one of the best salesmen. He used humor, and he understood the importance of his call—a soul might be in the balance. This was veteran publishing leader and literature evangelist, Bill Miller of Ocala, Florida. That lady now has the permanent and power-packed printed message books in her home. By using these human relation tactics or salesmanship, did Bill represent the ministry of Jesus? Do you think heaven approved of this method?

Anything that is moving forward, whether it be business or church, has some good salesperson behind it, unless the one in control can just dictate and those below him have no choice but to obey. However if choice and excellence are involved, it takes salesmanship. Every great leader is a great salesperson.

Throughout the four Gospels we see Jesus leading His followers step by step. "He gave us an example." DA, p. 24. "He was an example of what God designed all humanity to be through obedience to his laws." DA, p. 51. Jesus was our example in His human relationships. He understood how men think and how much of the truth He could give them at one time and how we are all led to any decision. "Step by step God leads His people." 1 T, p. 187. It is also true of humanity that when we go in the wrong direction, we never make a huge blunder at once. It has been the continual little steps that have led us there. "One false step leads to another." FE, p. 500.

Every professional sales book lists five steps of a sale. There may be some that will combine parts three and four. But these four or five steps are a part of every sales course taught. They are attention, interest, conviction, desire and close.

Let's look at how Jesus made a sales presentation and the fruit that was reaped because He took each step in the right sequence in John 4:7-42.

Step I, Attention (John 4:7, 8)

"A woman of Samaria came to draw water. Jesus said to her, 'Give Me a drink.' For His disciples had gone away into the city to buy food."

Step II, Interest (John 4:10-12)

"Then the women of Samaria said to Him, 'How is it You, being a Jew, ask a drink from me, a Samaritan woman? For Jews have no dealings with Samaritans.' Jesus answered and said to her, 'If you knew the gift of God, and who it is who says to you, give Me a drink, you would have asked Him, and He would have given you Living Water.' The woman said to Him, 'Sir, You have nothing to draw with, and the well is deep. Where then do You get that living water? Are you greater than our father Jacob, who gave us the well and drank from it himself, as well as his sons and his livestock?"

Step III, Conviction (John 4:13-15)

"Jesus answered and said to her, 'Whoever drinks of this water will thirst again, but whoever drinks of the water that I shall give him will never thirst. But the water that I shall give him will become in him a fountain of water springing up into ever-lasting life.' The woman said to Him, 'Sir, give me this water, that I may not thirst, nor come here to draw."

Step IV, Desire (John 4:16-24)

"Jesus said to her, 'Go, call your husband, and come here.' The woman answered and said, 'I have no husband.' Jesus said to her, 'You have well said, I have no husband, for you have had five husbands, and the one whom you now have is not your husband; in that you spoke truly.' The woman said to Him, 'Sir, I perceive that You are a prophet. Our fathers worshiped on this mountain, and you Jews say that in Jerusalem is the place where one ought to worship.' Jesus said to her, 'Woman, believe Me, the hour is coming when you will neither on this mountain, nor in Jerusalem, worship the Father. You worship what you do not know; we know what we worship, for salvation is of the Jews. But the hour is coming, and now is when the true worshipers will worship the Father in spirit and truth; for the Father is seeking such to worship Him. God is Spirit, and those who worship Him must worship in spirit and truth."

Step V, Action (Close of the Sale) (John 4:25-29)

"The woman said to Him, 'I know that Messiah is coming (who is called Christ). When He comes, He will tell us all things.' Jesus said to her, 'I who speak to you am He.' (And at this point His disciples came, and they marveled that He talked with a woman; yet no one said, 'What do you seek?' or, 'Why are You talking with her?') The woman then left her waterpot, went her way into the city, and said to the men, 'Come, see a Man who told me all things that I ever did. Could this be the Christ?' " Was Jesus a salesman? This is the first recorded sales presentation. Humanity's "Example" covered all five points. Ellen White says, "He reasoned more earnestly and eloquently with her than with kings, counselors or high priests. The lessons He gave to that woman have been repeated to the earth's remotest bounds." DA, p. 194, 195.

What was the result of this sale? (John 4:39-42)

"And many of the Samaritans of that city believed in Him because of the word of the woman who testified, 'He told me all that I ever did.' So when the Samaritans had come to Him, hey urged Him to stay with them; and He stayed there two days. And many more believed because of His own word. Then they said to the woman, 'Now we believe, not because of what you said, for we ourselves have heard Him and we know that this is indeed the Christ, the Savior of the world.' "

Chapter 3*

"For as he thinketh in his heart, so is he . . ."
Proverbs 23:7, KJV.

Attitude

Any psychologist will tell you that attitude has more to do with success, in any field, than does aptitude. Attitude is more important than natural abilities, education, heritage, wealth, or natural beauty. Almost invariably, when individuals are promoted, whether in the church or industry, attitude has more to do with promotion than do actual accomplishments. Although accomplishments usually follow a good attitude, it could be said that all wars are started by people with bad attitudes. In fact, "There was war in heaven" (Rev.12:7) that was started with one individual with a "bad attitude." Good attitudes win elections, change the course of a church, community or country. Good attitudes raise positive children. A good attitude creates an individual with qualities that win friends and inspire people.

If attitude is so important, why is it that so many are lacking in this area? How did we get the attitude that we have? How can we improve a bad attitude or maintain and grow an already posi-

---

* *I am indebted to the late Bill Higgins for some of the outline in the next five chapters. I became better acquainted with Elder Higgins during his last years. He helped me in training schools and was a real inspiration as well as a help to me. His ever present and sweet helpmate Genevieve, gave me his instruction material after his death. He is greatly missed.*

tive outlook. Zig Ziglar puts it this way, "You are what you are and where you are because of what has gone into your mind. You change what you are and where you are by changing what goes into your mind." Motivational author, Earl Nightingale said, "We are what we think about." Ellen White said, "Men become changed by beholding." COL, p. 355. Psychologist Will James said, "The greatest discovery of my generation is that human beings can alter their lives by altering their attitude of mind."

> "You change what you are and where you are by changing what goes into your mind." Zig Ziglar

If we want others to think positively about what we are doing, we must first have the right mental attitude. The following illustration depicts a man with a bad attitude and we meet people just like him. We are going to see what we can do through the next five chapters to change that attitude.

Because sin abounds on this planet many people may not appreciate your work when you first meet them. In America, we have what we call "Murphy's Law," which states, "If anything can go wrong, it will go wrong." Of course this is a negative way to view life. One man with a contrary attitude read this law and said, "I'm going to try and see if that is true." He took ten slices of bread, put peanut butter on one side and put them on a pan, and tossed them into the air. Nine of those slices fell face down with the peanut butter next to the floor sticking into his carpet. The tenth one stuck on the ceiling! He believes he proved Murphy's Law. But we are in a work that does not depend on chance. In our work "humanity lays hold upon divine power." CM, p. 104. With this combination, we are absolutely assured of success. It cannot fail. Now let us look at a number of things that will help you have a positive attitude.

1. Know Your Calling

The apostle Paul said, "Woe is unto me if I preach not the gospel!" 1 Cor. 9:16. "I was not disobedient unto the heavenly vision." Acts 26:19. Paul was called of God for a specific task. Paul saw the great need of humanity, and God showed him what he could do to fill that need. In fact, this is a definition of a call from God—to see the need and know that by God's grace you can fill that need. "Canvassers should be impressed with the fact that this is the very work that God would have them do." CM, p. 6. No question about it, problems will come. That should be expected. It is just par for the course. But a person with a positive attitude will surmount these difficulties and look back, thanking God for them.

> **A call from God is to see a need and know that by God's grace you can fill it.**

Brother Koni had a burden for his fellow men. He had spent many years working in the gold mines outside Johannesburg, South Africa. He lost his leg in a tragic mine accident and endured a limp brought on by an poorly fitted artificial limb. Although walking became a challenge thereafter, Brother Koni would become a literature evangelist whose only method of delivering the truth-filled books was walking and public transportation.

With the loss of his leg, Brother Koni could no longer work in the mines. He came to Soweto, a suburb of Johansburg, to work. There he found the Lord and the three angels' message. He had a burden for souls and was directed to publishing director, Pastor J. Lephatse. Brother Koni was soon taking books back to the same mines where he had worked. But as a literature evangelist, he was a different man from the rough miner that once passed through those guard gates.

Brother Koni was from the Xhosa tribe, but the mine guards were from another tribe which did not especially like his heritage. They were rough men and poorly educated. Brother Koni wanted to share with them the freedom he had found. They found this humorous. They scattered his books and threw him around. Of course this was not difficult with his artificial leg. They then beat him mercilessly. His head was so swollen that he could barely see out of the opening of his eyes. Miraculously, he found his way back to Pastor Lephatse's house in Soweto. Pastor Lephatse called me and shared what had happened. I got on my knees and prayed that God would help this very sincere man not to lose his faith and get discouraged. I was afraid that, as a relatively new Christian, he might think God had abandoned him. I did not believe he would ever sell books again ("Oh ye of little faith").

When brother Koni healed, he got another inventory of books and went back to that same mine where he was beaten! After the first year he had 5 baptisms, and he had more every year I was there. He was always a credentialed worker. He had more reasons not to do the Lord's work than most of us, but he heard God's call and responded.

Mike Courey who has sold more books in a single year in the Southern Union of the North American Division than any literature evangelist, said to me recently, "There is a reason for failure, and there is a reason for success. I know the results depend on the Lord and my working a consistent daily program. God has blessed me with the success I need to support my wife and five children." He has kept his children in church school and has given the last 15 years to the literature ministry. He says, " I'm absolutely convinced that I was born to be a literature evangelist." Mike's positive attitude about his calling is a big factor in his success. God will give that attitude to many more in the future. "In the closing work of the gospel, there is a vast field to be occupied; and, more than ever before, the work is to enlist helpers from the common people. Both the youth and those older in years will be called from the field, from the vineyard, and the workshop and sent forth by the Master. . . . If they will put their hearts into the work, and continue to be learners, He will fit them to labor for Him." CM p. 21

2. Set Goals

This is covered in detail in Chapter 10. Having a definite and reasonable objective to shoot for each day, week and year develops a positive attitude. As you measure your accomplishments against a standard you set, you have something to look forward to. Failure to reach a goal is not a person but an event, and is not to be taken personally. It does help us to understand where we are and where we need to improve.

3. Awake Positive

When you get up in the morning, greet the day with positive statements. Quote enthusiastically, Psalm 118:24, "This is the day which the Lord hath made; we will rejoice and be glad in it." This will help you set the pace for the day. Even your morning prayer and worship will have more zip if you do this. No matter what challenges you face, you will be more upbeat reminding yourself that God has given you this day.

4. Do Not Listen To Or Repeat Gossip Or Negative Talk

Rabbi Daniel Lapin in his publication, *Thought Tool*, has some profound thoughts in regard to this. "If we listen as others are maligned, in spite of our disinclination to believe what we hear, our relation with the vilified individual is forever altered. In other words, we are involuntarily influenced by everything we hear. Harmless gossip does not exit. Listening to gossip will usually leave us feeling less worthy. Words penetrate to our souls and cannot be erased or ignored.

"Leviticus 19:14 says, 'Thou shalt not curse a deaf man.' Since he can not hear what harm has been done, the prohibition is due to the effect on the curser himself. He hears his own words and they reduce his worth as a human being."

Ellen White has counsel on this also. "He [Satan] stands by to excite the mind and make the most of the advantage gained. He knows that all this gossip and talebearing and revealing of secrets and dissecting of character separates the soul from God. It is death to spiritually and a calm religious influence." *Mind, Character, and Personality*, p. 779.

5. Praise Other People and God Audibly

Rabbi Lapin's counsel on this is: "Overcome your inhibitions about talking to yourself. Prepare speeches by actually saying them out loud. A winning mind-set is the consequence of hearing words that penetrate right to the core of personality.

"If we truly wish to believe something, we should tell it to ourselves audibly, rather than thinking it silently.

"Since we remember far better that which we hear, reading aloud increases our vocabulary, fluency, and range of ideas. Above all, it inspires.

"Each time you say something good about someone in your life, you increasingly believe it yourself.

"Self-censorship benefits one's soul. Since everything that enters the mind through the ears has an effect, it is better not to hear certain things.

"Through speech one can substantially increase inner feelings of harmony and satisfaction with certain unchangeable facts of one's life. Praising God makes a close relationship with Him. This is part of the basis for praying out loud."

6. Listen

A good attitude enables one to listen to others. God calls and God equips as people apply themselves. I dislike the expression, "He's a born salesman." What most people mean when they say this is that a person who talks on and on can convince others to buy. But let me assure you that this does not make a salesman—especially a literature evangelist. I do not believe a person is a "born salesperson" any more than there are born doctors or lawyers. Your work is a calling and the skills that you need to be successful are learned. Listening is a learned skill. I have worked with some of the most successful literature evangelists in America and Africa as well as the champion colporteur, Andre Loots, of Kazakhstan in the former Soviet Union. What I've observed is that all of these people are good listeners, and they speak at the appropriate time. I worked with a lady who led the Southern Union of the Trans-Africa Division in sales for years. One of the things that impressed me about Joyce Motea was that she was a good listener. She knew how to make others feel good about themselves.

> **Your work is a calling, and the skills that you need to be successful are learned. Listening is a learned skill.**

Lonnie Kerbs canvassed for many summers then went on to become a leading literature evangelist and is now one of our successful publishing leaders. He told me that when he was a student and had not learned the skills of good listening, one woman got his attention. The lady whom he was canvassing suspected that he was an Adventist and wanted to see what he believed about the state of the dead. She asked him, "Young man, do you believe in hell?" (Lonnie, being young and inexperienced and maybe a little nervous, thought she meant heaven.) He answered, "Yes ma'am, I sure do, and I'm looking forward to going there!" The lady exclaimed in a loud voice, "I said Hell! Hell!" Obviously, Lonnie overcame this problem of listening, but this story illustrates a point. Listening to a prospect is as important as what we say in making a gospel sales presentation. Knowing when to listen, when to talk and what to say are learned skills.

Here are four ways to be a more effective listener:

1) Make eye contact. Nothing is more demeaning than looking at your watch when someone is talking to you. It shows your mind is somewhere else. Make eye contact, show you are really interested in what they have to say. They are the most important person in the world for the time you are with them. Good eye contact does not mean you stare them down. The other extreme is the person who looks over your shoulder while talking to you.

2) Acknowledge their main points with statements like; "I agree with that," "that is a good point," "you are right," "that is interesting." Acknowledge their point with an open ended question using either the words, *how, why, what, when* or *where* in your question. Acknowledgment can be read also with a smile or nod of the head.

3) Restate what they have said occasionally. Especially when a statement is made that will make a point you want to bring up later in your presentation.

4) Use positive body language. Face the prospect and sit erect.

Sitting erect shows you are alive and interested in them. Never lean back in a chair and never sit with your arms crossed. Psychologist tell us that if you sit with your arms crossed it makes the other person feel you are closed to their opinion.

7. Health

If you're going to have a good attitude, you must have good health. There's a definite relationship between our physical well-being and our mental attitude. More and more medical scientists are discovering the connection between health and attitude. The brain needs good food and a fresh supply of oxygen continually. If we eat the proper food, get the proper exercise and get adequate rest, then we stand a much better chance of having a positive attitude. "The state of the mind has largely to do with the health of the body." CF, p. 375.

Let us imagine for a moment that you have a very rich uncle. He dies suddenly and you are remembered in his will. He has left you with a new Rolls Royce and a race horse worth 10 million dollars. How would you take care of these gifts? Would you put kerosene in the Rolls Royce or the finest grade gasoline? Would you keep the race horse up all hours of the night watching television? Of course not. But how about the rich gift our heavenly Father has given has given each of you in this tremendous machine, the human body? What a wonderful gift it is. Every breath we take is a miracle, but so many professing to believe in our health message do abuse this gift in a like manner described above.

The great football coach, Vince Lombardi, once said, "Fatigue causes fear." If we have fear when we go out to do God's work, it may be because we have not rested properly. Elijah, the great prophet, became afraid at a time when he was tired and worn out. It was after he ate and rested and then ate and rested again, that God spoke to him and gave him more instruction as to his important ministry.

The most celebrated baseball player in modern history is Mickey Mantle. Mickey Mantle was loved by everyone, but he had a fatalistic attitude and didn't see himself living for a long time because his father died young. He acquired many bad habits that caused his health to deteriorate early. A famous quote he made in jest reflects what many people think after they have wasted their health, "If I had known that I was going to live this long, I would have taken better care of myself." Mickey, that likable personality, shortened his career and his life because of some of his habits. On the other hand is Dave Winfield, not as popular and who may not have accomplished as much in the short term, but he played many more years. On his recent retirement, he said, "I've played longer than others because when others were doing things that hurt their bodies, I took care of my health."

Being a successful literature evangelist requires energy. Generally the amount of energy we have will be in direct proportion to the care we give our bodies.

8. Cleanliness

It has been said that clean clothing is a source of moral power, second only to that of a clean conscience. If you feel comfortable, if you feel clean, if your clothes are clean and your grooming appears neat and clean, you will definitely have a better attitude. When you leave in the morning and you have had a good shower, have on a clean shirt, your pants look pressed, your shoes are shined, your tie is tied correctly and your hair is groomed, it just makes you feel like you're going to have a good day. It makes you feel like you are going to have good thoughts today! You are ready! Clean clothes, even a clean car is important. Elder Higgins used to tell us that he thought our car would even run better when it's clean! Well, it may not run any better, but it will seem like it does to us, and that will effect the way that we think about ourselves. If we pull into a driveway and our car is covered with mud and has papers scattered over the interior, our prospect may be wondering, "Where did that disaster happen?"

9. Dress

The clothes, the dress that you wear, not only will affect the attitude of other people about you, but it will affect your own attitude about other people. It's better to buy good quality clothes that fit well and wear longer. They make you look like a successful person. People do not like to deal with failures. They like to deal with successful people. Do all within your means to look successful.

Often the difference between success and failure is just a little thing. Let's do all we can to make sure that we have that positive attitude. You'll stand taller if know you are properly dressed, well groomed and your shoes are shined.

The late Joe Hunt, another mentor of mine, used to tell the story about the literature evangelist who went to the door with unpressed baggy pants. They even bulged out around the knees. One lady who came to the door, looked at his pants and said, "Mister, if you're going to jump, jump!" An image consultant told me that we only have twenty seconds to make a first impression. Let's make sure it's a positive one.

10. Knowledge

Knowledge gives confidence. If you know your product, you have more confidence. If you've read the material in your books, it gives you confidence. You need a disciplined plan before you start every day. Read something from the books that you sell.

In the nineteenth century when wagon trains were going west, there was a valley, sometimes very muddy, that had to be crossed. Someone erected a sign at the beginning of the valley that read "Choose your rut wisely because you will be in it for the next twelve miles." If we are in a rut let us be sure it is a positive one. Know what you are going to say.

Memorize a canvass. Memorizing your presentation will do more to helping you get the right start than probably any other single factor. Why memorize? Some people like to say, "I just want to be myself. I don't want a canned presentation. That presentation is just not me." Can you imagine a movie star who makes millions, when given a script to an important movie, telling the director and producer, "I can't memorize these lines. These lines are just not me?" When you memorize a canvass, it does many things for you.

1) It gives you a place to start.

2) It gives you a place to finish.

3) It gives you a close that works.

4) It is organized and has been prepared by others who have been successful.

5) It gives you a place to restart when interrupted (and all of us will be interrupted at times when we are making a presentation in someone's home).

There is absolutely no substitute for knowledge. Someone has said, "You cannot tell what you do not know anymore than you can leave where you did not go." We should be like the artesian well that bubbles up and flows with beautiful clear water, refreshing and wholesome. It's what you know about your product that will give power, conviction and enthusiasm to what you say.

If you have memorized an 18-minute presentation and that is all that you know about these books, you are not going to have an attitude of success. Many successful literature evangelists will tell you that they give only a 17 to 18 minute presentation, but they know enough about the books that they could talk for hours.

When I worked in the Florida Conference, I visited with a literature evangelist who wasn't making it. I wasn't in his home long before I found out why. Instead of having the whole set of the books that he sold, he only had the three that he used in demonstrating. He didn't own a set of the books that he was asking others to buy. He had not read the books himself!

You want to give power to your presentation? Look your customer in the eye and say, "You know, here is a paragraph I love from this book, *Desire of Ages*." Or, "This morning, I was reading this book and I read this text again that I love so much. . ." and share it with them. Share a part of a story that you have read recently or that you've read with your children and say, "Isn't that a beautiful story? If your child just read this one story, it would be worth the price of this whole set!" When you are fired with fresh enthusiasm because of a discovery you've made in your own books, it will help you to do something special.

Be a specialist. Knowledge of your material will make you a specialist. The story is told about a man who was called to a factory to fix a machine. He looked at the machine, took out a hammer, hit the machine in the right place and the machine was fixed. He gave the man in charge a bill. The bill was for $1,000. The factory foreman said, "You had better itemize this. How could you charge me $1,000 for what you did?" The specialist said, "Okay," and wrote the following: "Hitting with a hammer—$1.00; knowing where to hit with the hammer—$999!" You see, he was a specialist. He knew what to do and even though it only took ten minutes, the factory was willing to pay for his expertise. When you're a specialist, you'll have a winning attitude. One lady who sold many copies of *Great Controversy*, said that what gave her power in selling this book was that she read that book through on her knees every year.

A few years ago, one of our literature evangelists had to have heart surgery. It cost $50,000. A heart surgeon can put a new heart in a person today. They are specialists and can charge a great deal. You, as a literature evangelist, may be in a home for only 30 minutes but you can put a new heart in a person if you do the right things and have the knowledge that you need. You may not charge $50,000 but you can give that person a heart that will carry him into eternity.

11. People's Needs

If you're going to have the right attitude, you must see the needs of people today. There is a great need, and you can fulfill it. Every individual will reach someone that no one else can reach. There are so many problems in homes. You only have to read your newspaper to see it today. There is heartache, divorce, crime—stories which are all too familiar.

We must pray to God that He will give us the wisdom of knowing how to meet the needs of people with a few words in the short time that we are in front of them. You bring to many people the only ray of hope they will see. So many times customers have told me, "I never let anyone in my home. I don't know why I let you in." We know why. Angels attend this work. People have told me that they were going to commit suicide the day that I called, but because God blessed my visit, my book and my prayer, their lives have been changed.

"A soft answer turneth away wrath; but grievous words stir up anger." Proverbs 15:1. We must cultivate the ability to reach people with all these special needs. I heard a story once about a pastor who met a man in a store. The man was gruff, spoke angrily and was rude. The pastor said to him, as he looked him in the eye, "Sir, you must be carrying heavy burdens." The man looked at the pastor and said, "You know, I am" and began to weep. He said, "Yesterday, we got a letter from the government telling us that our son had been killed in Viet Nam." This pastor was able to minister to that man's needs. Yes, there are so many people with needs, and we can show them the way to a better life. When we truly understand this, it will affect our attitude.

12. Prayer

Our personal prayer life will affect our attitude. There is an old saying that "Prayer changes things." We can also say that prayer changes people. And I believe we can say prayer changes thinking—prayer will change attitudes. Prayer will do wonders. My mother was not a Seventh-day Adventist, but she read her Bible daily and she prayed. I remember when I first went away to college and was not attending church, I had an experience that

I can't explain. I felt someone was praying for me, and I'm sure it was my mother. I remember getting on my knees that day and praying. Later I received a letter from my mother saying that she felt concerned for me and had been praying for me. Prayer does things that we can't explain. It changes people. It changes attitudes.

"Prayer will give to the voice persuasive power." GW, p. 510. One customer said of a literature evangelist, "That man was in my house for less than 30 minutes and I felt like I had been to church." Another said after a literature evangelist prayed in his home, "You know my preacher comes over and has a chicken dinner occasionally, but he has never prayed for me like you have."

Pray each day that God will give you the spiritual armor described in Ephesians 6:12-20. We are in a spiritual war. Be sure the enemy will have some "fiery darts" [verse 16] made just for you. Put "Your shield of faith" up and you will only hear a ping as it glances off, and you keep marching forward.

13. Work

"Work and pray, work and pray." CM, p. 81. "Prayer can never take the place of duty." COL , p. 143 Prayer is so very important but after we've prayed, we must go to work. I remember talking with a literature evangelist who wasn't having the success that he needed. When I went to see him he told me, "You know, I spent all day yesterday praying." I told him he needed to have time for prayer, but he would never take an order just praying. Seldom will people come to us. The gospel commission says, "Go." "The secret of success is the union of divine power with human effort." CM, p. 106. When on my knees, I have received power for my work, but I have never written up a sales contract on my knees. I had to go out! "Then the master said to the servant, 'Go out to highways and hedges.'" Luke 14:23. When we work hard, our work is easy, but when we work easy, our work is hard.

> **"The secret of success is the union of divine power with human effort." Colporteur Ministry, p. 106**

One of the best remedies for depression whether financial or mental is work. If you have problems, work. If you have difficulties at home, work. If you don't have the amount of sales you want, work. God can only bless those who work. Hard work gives us a feeling of security. A person who does not work hard seldom has a positive attitude. "More than natural endowments, . . . habits . . . decide . . . the battles of life." DA, p. 101. If you have a big day already by 2 p.m., don't quit, work more, have a bigger day! This is what champions do!

"Character cannot be developed in ease and quiet. Only through experiences of trial and suffering can the soul be strengthened, vision cleared, ambition inspired and success achieved."—Helen Keller

God wants us to prosper financially. He wants us to pay a good tithe and offerings. He wants us to be examples in our local churches. People who don't work usually have a guilt complex. Remember that the stars always come out at night. "All day Jesus ministered to those who came to Him; in the evening He gave attention to such as through the day, must toil to earn a pittance for support of their families." GW, p. 42.

Two literature evangelists lived in the same town in a western state. One had more ability than the other. But the one with lesser ability always worked harder or at least longer hours. When he was in the part of the city where the more talented one lived, he would pass his friend's house on the way home. As he crossed a bridge, he could look down at the apartment of his friend and see his car sitting in the driveway. He knew that almost every day he made at least one more call than his friend. The more talented one eventually became discouraged. The less talented one became discouraged, too, but seemed to always overcome it by his hard work. God used both men, but the one who worked harder was consequently asked to go to mission service and had the privilege of serving in many places. He always felt that his friend was more qualified. The difference seemed to be in their work habits. Their challenges were not different:

1) They lived in the same city.

2) They served the same God.

3) They sold the same books.

The more talented one did work several years, but eventually discouragement overcame him and he left the literature ministry. The difference appeared to be work habits. "We are what we repeatedly do. Excellence, this is not an act, but a habit." Aristotle.

> "We are what we repeatedly do. Excellence, this is not an act, but a habit." Aristotle

14. Overcome Fear

Fear is the following

F alse
E vidence
A ppearing
R eal

One way to overcome fear is by claiming Bible promises. One author claims to have found 365 promises that say, "fear not," or "fear ye not." That is one for every day of the year. "Those who work for God will meet with discouragement, but the promise is always theirs; 'Lo I am with you always even to the end of the world.' *Matthew 28:20*. God will give a most wonderful experience to those who will say I believe thy promise and I will not fail nor become discouraged." CM, p. 115. Former General Conference Publishing Director, Elder Bruce Wickwire used to tell of an Asian man named Lo, who came to him and said "Elder Wickwire, I found God's special promise to me, '*Lo*, I am with you always." *Matthew 28:20*. It is also my promise and yours. "Bill, I am with you always."

Elder Joe Hunt told an experience from East Africa of a literature evangelist traveling between villages on a bicycle. He sold a large order to a man in a village near the road and delivered the books. He continued going down the road and that evening he started back home. As he came near the house where he had sold the large order, his good customer saw him and came running out toward the road. The literature evangelist tried to ignore the man and continued peddling looking straight ahead. He was sure this man was going to cancel that big order. He thought if he could just ignore him and go right on by, the man would forget about it. But as he looked back, he saw the man jump on a bicycle and begin chasing him. The literature evangelist peddled faster and faster. The man behind him peddled faster and faster. As the literature evangelist was becoming exhausted, he looked back and saw this man gaining ground on him. Just before the man caught him, the literature evangelist stopped, knowing he was going to have to take his books back. The customer said, "My, you are hard to catch. You must come back and see some of my neighbors. They have seen my books and they want some also." Often we fear the worst which seldom comes true.

15. Keep A Sense Of Humor

I have observed that people who can laugh at their mistakes and mishaps enjoy their work and other people much more. They know the direction they are going and have developed a healthy self-image. On the other hand people who cannot laugh at their own mistakes are usually uptight, sensitive, and have few real friends. These people simply do not enjoy life as much. They have a harder time taking directions and praising others on their work. A healthy sense of humor will help us weather storms, and we will be happier, healthier, and more prosperous literature evangelist.

Will Rogers said, "Most people are about as happy as they make up their mind to be." The Scriptures tell us, "...He that is of a merry heart has a continual feast." Proverbs 15:15. None of us has a pain free life but God gives all enough joys to enjoy this life and our special mission. A healthy sense of humor helps to create a good attitude.

Remember that the sun always shines brighter in the morning just after the darkest hour. All of us have trials and set backs. All of us come to Christ with some baggage. None of us had perfect parents, church or neighbors. But by God's grace we can become positive. Heaven will be a positive place, and the Lord wants us to practice for heaven here. He will help you to have a positive attitude. Attitude is not inherited, it is learned. It is a choice we make. Follow the steps in this chapter and you will have a positive attitude!

Chapter 4

"How beautiful upon the mountains are the feet of him that publisheth peace; that bringeth good tidings of good, that publisheth salvation; that saith unto Zion; Thy God reigneth!" Isaiah 52:7, KJV.

Sell Yourself First

E very person you meet is forming an opinion of you. That opinion weighs heavily on their decision whether to accept you into their home and whether to buy your truth-filled books. We want to do all we can to sell ourselves to the prospect, and in selling ourselves, to sell the gospel of Jesus Christ.

At our office, we get many letters from people who really appreciate the literature evangelists who call on them. But occasionally we received a letter from someone who does not appreciate the manner in which our representative carried himself. In one letter that came to our office, the lady wrote, "I love the books, and I want them for my family. But I refuse to buy them from the man who called at my home. If you have someone who represents your company in a more wholesome way, please send him to my home and I will buy these books." We sent someone else, and she did buy the books. Unfortunately, most people are not that determined. Do not allow the balance to tip in favor of Satan because of something that you do. When you represent the Lord in a home, the Holy Spirit will begin to touch the hearts of the people and they will see something in you that they do not see anywhere else.

One representative told this story. He had finished his presentation, made the sale and had prayer in the home. The phone rang at the very moment that he had finished his prayer. The lady excused herself, answered the phone and told the party on the other end, "May I call you back? My minister is here now." She said, after hanging up, that never had anyone come into her home who represented the Lord to her as did this literature evangelist.

Let's look at some things that will help us sell ourselves first.

1. Character

Character is what you are. Character creates an atmosphere. Just being good does good. It is said that Dwight L. Moody could walk into a barber shop where people were accustomed to telling crude jokes, and his very presence would change the atmosphere of that barber shop into the atmosphere of a church. Character is power.

"Every soul is surrounded by an atmosphere of its own,—an atmosphere, it may be, charged with the life-giving power of faith, courage, and hope, and sweet with the fragrance of love. Or it may be heavy and chilled with the gloom of discontent and selfishness, or poisonous with the deadly taint of cherished sin. By the atmosphere surrounding us, every person with whom we come in contact is consciously or unconsciously affected." CM, pp. 67, 68.

Character gives you belief in yourself. Numbers 13 is the famous spy chapter. Any Bible student can tell you this story. They can tell you the names of the people who brought back the positive report after spying out Canaan. The positive, or the minority, reports were those of Joshua and Caleb. There were 12 spies and all their names were given, but very few people can tell you the names of the other ten. Joshua and Caleb had character. They believed in their mission and they saw things as God saw them.

Tennyson had one of his literary characters, Sir Galahad, make this statement, "My strength is as the strength of ten thousand because my heart is pure." I like that—character. His heart was pure, and it gave him character. Aristotle said, "The single greatest force in persuasion is the character of the speaker."

> "Men of genius are ordained. Men of wealth are envied. Men of power are feared, but men of character are trusted." Arthur Friedman.

2. Be Punctual

Many seem to find it difficult to be on time. This costs sales and souls. Not many things are more frustrating than waiting on someone who does not value your time or theirs. There is a ripple effect of time lost that is multiplied by the number of people waiting on one tardy person. Being late shows disrespect for those waiting and is a sign of disorganization. A sure way to lose a sale is to be late.

Dr. Allan Zimmerman, professor and seminar speaker suggests a way to break this habit. The next time you are late to an appointment, announce to those waiting, "I am a total incompetent and have no control over my life." This may seem a little extreme, but his point is good.

3. Love the People

If we're going to sell ourselves, we must love others. Sometimes we meet people who have some unlovely traits. They may even be a little rude or crude. But we must look at them as someone for whom Christ died on Calvary. You must look at people through the eyes of Jesus. If someone says something to you that hurts your feelings when you are at the door or in the home, remember that you are Christ's ambassador and they did not say it to you—they said it to Jesus. Never take negative statements personally. You are Christ's ambassador! Sometimes the people who may appear the least likely to receive your material and the least friendly at the time you start your presentation may be the very ones who will purchase your books and share eternity with you.

Many of us have sold books to people and later saw those people baptized. At the time we were making the presentation, we may have wondered whether we were wasting our time. But because we were Christ's ambassadors, we made a full presentation, and God blessed our effort.

One of our General Conference leaders told of a young man who worked in Latin America. This young man knocked on the door and a lady answered, upset that she was interrupted in the middle of her meal. The young man was persuasive, but she didn't want to hear what he had to say so she threw her half glass of milk right in his face. The resourceful young man licked his lips, paused for a moment and smiled. Then looking at her he said, "That does taste good. May I have some more?" The lady laughed, her heart was softened and the young man was invited into her home. He left with an order and started Bible studies. Six months later, she was a member of the Seventh-day Adventist Church.

Love finds a way. "Love will open doors and hearts," CM, p. 55. Yes, love will find a way. I think we should pray everyday, "Lord, help me even to love the dogs." I have a feeling that even a dog knows if you love him or not. A dog can look in your face and see if you have a kind face before he bites you on the heel. I've only been bitten by a dog one time in all of my years in the literature ministry. And I think that little pug-nose bulldog totally misunderstood! The old adage, "People don't care how much you know until they know how much you care" is so true. How much you care is reflected in the tone of your voice and the look on your face. Love truly is the most powerful force in the world. When people like you, the sale is one-third made before they ever see the book. Dale Carnegie said, "Make a friend and sell a friend."

When I worked in the Colorado Conference, a literature evangelist shared with me how loving the people not only made a sale but brought someone into the church. He made a call on a home where there was a mother, a teenage girl and a baby. As he canvassed the family, he assumed the baby belonged to the middle-aged mother. But the baby was the child of the teenage girl. The family began to open their hearts because they could see that this literature evangelist truly had love for them. In this little farm community, this girl had a child out of wedlock, and the local church she attended had ridiculed her. They called her unfit. As in all small, close knit communities, gossip travels fast and she felt everyone was talking about her. As she told her story, she began crying. She told of her guilt and embarrassment. Our literature evangelist told her about the story of Jesus forgiving the woman who was caught in adultery and how she became an important part of the gospel story. As he talked with this family, he was able to invite this young girl to accept Jesus as her personal Savior. The family purchased the children's literature and a message book. Later, there was an evangelistic meeting held nearby. This young girl was invited by the literature evangelist and was baptized into the Seventh-day Adventist Church. At her baptism, she gave this testimony, "It is so wonderful to know Jesus and that He accepts people regardless of the mess they have made of their lives."

> **Treat the duke and the ditch digger the same—treat them both like a duke.**

4. Courtesy and Cheerfulness

Courtesy is one of the graces of the Spirit. Courtesy comes from the word "court." It means how you conduct yourself in court—in royal court! In royal court, you're courteous to all. Someone said you ought to treat the duke and the ditch digger the same—you treat them both like a duke. Courtesy is how you meet people, how you shake hands with people, your manners, eye contact, and how you listen. Always try to make the other person feel important. When you shake hands, let people know that they have grabbed hold of a human being who has a heart on the other end of his arm. Do not crush their hand, but show that you are glad to see them. Put a little enthusiasm into your handshake not just a limp hand on the end of a dead arm.

Someone has said: Hearts like doors will open—
With little—very little keys.
Two of these are
"Thank you friend" and "If you please."

If you please where you go, you can go where you please. The very first thing that you say when you step into someone's home, because you are there at their invitation, is "thank you." When you are seated, say "thank you" — "Thank you very kindly." Courtesy in human relations is like oiling the machinery. It keeps down the friction. Literature evangelists should be the most courteous people in the world.

"There is a great lack of true politeness among us as a people." 4T, p. 392. "If we give smiles, they will be returned to us; if we speak pleasant, cheerful words, they will be spoken to us again." AH, p. 430. "God's people are to catch the reflection of the smile of God, and reflect it to others. They are to see how much sunshine they can bring into the lives of those around them." MM, p. 45. "There is no smile that He does not mark." SC, p. 86. Some people don't realize it, but it takes four times more muscles to frown than to smile. It is much easier to smile, and it will do a g-r-e-a-t deal in helping us to sell ourselves.

"There is no cosmetic for beauty like happiness," Said Lady Blessington. "Let us learn from Christ how to combine a high sense of purity and integrity with sunniness of disposition." CM, pp. 72, 73.

Christ wasn't sad looking. How do we know that? Because the children wanted to come to Him, and children only come to people who are relaxed and happy. When you get people to smile, you get them to relax. Bruce Wickwire, of the General Conference, used to always say, "When you go out to work, always put on your east-west smile." Zig Ziglar says in his sales book, "Smile like you can eat a banana sideways." Remember what the image consultant told me, "You only have 20 seconds to make a first impression." Smile even if at times you do not feel like it. In a recent survey it was reported that waitresses who smiled got 30 percent more tips than those who did not, and doctors who did not smile had twice as many malpractice suits.

5. Dress

Image consultants tell us that when people look at you, there are a few main areas where they will look as they size you up! For men 1) the color of your shirt, 2) your tie, and 3) your shoes. For ladies, the four items that they see first are 1) the hair, 2) the neckline, 3) the hemline, and 4) the shoes. In selling yourself, the way that you dress will say a great deal about how people perceive you. I heard a criminal psychologist speak who said he would get a description of a criminal who had left the scene. As people described what the criminal wore, his hair and anything else that could be remembered about him, the psychologist could draw a pretty accurate profile of the individual. Dress has a great deal to say about selling ourselves. "It [your appearance] affects your influence over others for time and eternity." CM, p.65.

This applies to the car you drive. If you live in a country where you ride a bicycle or motorcycle, the condition in which you keep your mode of transportation still applies. It also applies to the samples in your briefcase. All of these should reflect professionalism, so that you make a good first impression.

6. Health

If you are going to sell yourself, you need good health. A radiant happy, healthy person attracts people. All of us enjoy being around somebody who is healthy and enthusiastic. This is the reason that you should be careful about your diet and exercise. Start every day with an invigorating breakfast. Amazingly, many of our people do not do this and yet talk about the health message. A good breakfast fosters an attitude of optimism and cheerfulness which sets the pace, psychologically, for the day's activities. Usually people who wait to noon till eat a meal are more prone to mood swings. Your body needs good fuel to start the day. Someone who is moody, sickly or complaining about their ailments, will not attract other people. You need energy if you are going to appeal to people and sell them.

The next item under health may seem obvious, but everyone may face the problem of offensive breath or body odor. Recently, I went to a meeting and met a man who was a professional and was very successful. Yet he had no idea of how his halitosis was offending those with whom he talked. He was friendly and would get right in your face when talking. His breath was so foul, I think I could have smelled it if he were talking with me over the phone! Whatever he had to say, most people wouldn't stay around to hear. A rule of human nature is that you cannot antagonize people and influence them favorably at the same time. Always carry a breath freshener or even a toothbrush. Stop and brush your teeth during the day. Use a deodorant that works for you. This may seem like a simple statement, but it is one that is violated so often by people who are professionals. One medical report states that eight out of every ten people will offend someone with halitosis at times. As one sales trainer said, "Do not let your breath enter before you do."

7. Know your business

"Our very prayers should be, Lord, help me to do my best. Teach me how to do better work. Give me energy and cheerfulness. Help me to bring into my work the loving ministry of the Savior." MH, p. 474. In selling yourself, there is no substitute for knowing. It matters not how old or young, how thin or fat, how short or tall you are, if you know your business, and really know it, the world will stand aside and salute you. Be a specialist, know your business.

8. Tact

Ask the right questions and get the right answers. Being tactful is asking the right questions. I will never forget an experience that taught me to ask more tactful questions. I was a young literature evangelist and had received a lead card at an address of a beautiful mansion. I arrived at the home early in the morning. The lady who answered the door was wearing work clothes, and had a shock of red hair that shot in every direction. Something in her hand gave the appearance that she was cleaning the house. She was abrupt when she answered the door and she startled me. I couldn't think of what to say. I blurted out, "Are you the maid?" She looked back at me and said, "I knew I looked like ___, but I didn't think I looked that bad." Needless to say, I did not get in that home. I had not yet learned how to ask the right questions. It would have been so much better if I had said with a question mark in my voice, "Mrs. Jones?" and waited for her answer.

Sometimes you may use some holy imagination. Annalisa Helavera of Finland, who led the world field for many years, worked in a very secular society. Many of the people she contacted were atheists, communists or very secular Christians. She once knocked on a door, and a man answered. Upon finding the nature of her business, he said "I hate Christians. I wish they would all leave." Annalisa replied, "They are, they are all going to leave, I've got to tell you about it!" He let her in and she sold him a *Great Controversy*.

One of the challenges in the western world today is how to get people to turn off the television while you are making your presentation. People will have a television blaring and not even know it's on. As Elder Higgins used to say, "It babbles like their mad cousin." I like to ask people, "Am I interfering with your favorite TV program?" If they don't get the hint and turn it either down or off, I may say, "You know, those guys are professionals, and I'm not. Would you mind turning it down while I show this material briefly? Thank You." Pray to God for wisdom and always be tactful.

9. Be Observant

Find something in their home or on their person that will help you pay them a sincere compliment. The world is starving to death for the lack of appreciation. Psychologist Will James said, "The single greatest urge of a human being is the desire to be appreciated." Dale Carnegie said, "Everybody is wearing a sign stating 'Make me feel important.'" People may have a beautiful car or garden, a picture of their children, a trophy, a neat and clean house. There is an old saying, "Take a child by the hand and you take the mother by the heart." I have found that to be true in my experience. There is always something for which we can pay a sincere compliment. They may have an oriental rug on their floor that costs $30,000. What does the Bible say? "Where your treasure is, there will be your heart also." Matt. 6:21.

> **"The single greatest urge of a human being is the desire to be appreciated." Will James**

I was working with David Tucker, a literature evangelist in Kansas. We called on a home in the country. An elderly lady was home, but she said she was too busy and did not have time to talk with us. I explained to her that we had traveled quite far to find her farm and our call would be brief if she would just take a few minutes. She again told me that she just didn't have time. As I thanked her and looked around, I saw a yard full of beautiful roses. I said, "You know, Mrs. Kennedy, you or someone here really has a green thumb! Someone has the gift for growing beautiful roses. You have so many!" This disarmed her and she began to talk. Ah, I had found what was her treasure. She took us through her roses and explained the different varieties. I learned things I never heard before about roses. She must have taken 10 or 15 minutes to tell us about her roses. As she had finished, I looked at her again and said, "You know ma'am, we've traveled quite far to see you today. Would you take just a few minutes and look at these while we are here? Only your interest will keep us longer." She invited us into her home. You see, we had set her at ease by being interested in her hobby and we had listened to her. She told us, as she looked at our beautiful books and as we talked about Christ's second coming, how much she believed Jesus was coming soon. She was concerned that her church no longer preached the Bible-based message that it once did. She was concerned about her grand-children, and what they were learning. She also told us that she had cancer and only had six months to live. As we shared our material with her, the Holy Spirit had time to work on her heart and impressed her that this was exactly what she needed. She purchased a set of children's books with a message book for each of her two sets of grandchildren and paid cash. We left praising the Lord. But this sale would never have happened had we not given her a sincere compliment on what was near to her heart. We helped her feel appreciated, and the balance was tipped toward eternity for two families and all who may read those books.

"Jesus... made Himself familiar with their interests and their occupations, that He might gain access to their hearts." MH, pp. 24, 25. By buying these books, what she really said was, "These men are nice, they were interested in me, and I like them. They made me feel important today." Remember, every person you meet is wearing an invisible badge that says, "Please make me feel important today."

In chapter two we have a model sales presentation that Jesus gave the women at the well. Sections eight and nine of this chapter tell how to accomplish step one of that sales presentation. Lets look what happened in the sale described above and note:

1) *Attention*

We got her attention by observing her treasured roses and showing genuine interest in them.

2) *Interest*

We got her interest by pointing out the needs of young people and the importance of getting back to the Bible. This was her great concern.

3) *Conviction*

She knew that now was the time as she didn't have long to live and her grandchildren were growing so fast.

4) *Desire*

She desired something that would help her pass on her beliefs to her grandchildren. Our literature was the answer.

5) *Close*

This was not difficult in this case, but would never have happened had we not first accomplished steps one through four, especially step one.

10. Show interest

Tim Leffew and James Byrd called on a gentleman in central Kentucky. As they were entering the home, James saw a picture of the man of the house in a World War II uniform with war decorations. He asked the gentleman where he had served. After the elderly gentleman responded, James said, "I want to thank you for what you did for our country." The gentleman got tears in his eyes and said, "No one ever has said that to me before." That sincere compliment was powerful! And now he was their friend and eager to hear what they had to say. Once you have observed the customer and see what their interests are, log it in your memory. If you don't use this to set them at ease, it may come in handy when you are closing and looking for another reserve point. Remember that every person you meet is superior to you in some way.

Is what I have said "just selling" or "just good public relations" or is it based on Bible principle? Listen to what the apostle Paul says in 1 Cor. 9:20-22, LB, "When I'm with the Jews, I seem as one of them so that they will listen to the gospel and I can win them to Christ. When I'm with Gentiles who follow Jewish customs, in ceremonies I don't argue, even if I don't agree, because I want to help them. When with the heathen, I agree with them as much as I can, except of course that I must always do what is right as a Christian. And so, by agreeing, I can win their confidence and help them too. When I am with those whose consciences bother them easily, I don't act as though I know it all and don't say they are foolish; the result is that they are willing to let me help them. Yes, whatever a person is like, I try to find common ground with him so that he will let me tell him about Christ and let Christ save him." When you have done the things mentioned in these last two chapters, your sale is one-third made. Now the man we looked at earlier is beginning to change his mind.

Chapter 5

"The grass withereth, the flower fadeth:
but the word of our God shall stand forever."
Isaiah 40:8, KJV.

The Approach

Let's look again at this man's brain. This man we mentioned earlier has been changing some of his thoughts. He was fearful and suspicious. Now after you have sold yourself, suddenly he is trusting, and this is a tremendous victory. When you've sold yourself and the prospective customer trusts you, the sale is one-third made, and you haven't even shown a book yet. Success is 75 percent preparation. In warfare, they say successful battles are thought out before they are fought out. You must know in advance what you are going to do. Now we will look at what comprises a successful approach.

1. Information

The more information that you have about prospects when you call on them, the more likely you are to make sales. This is especially true when you are running referrals. A referral is a prospect that has been referred to you. Often customers or neighbors will give you information about the person they are referring. They'll tell you what church they attend, where they work, the age of their children and when is the best time to catch them home. The most important item to get right is the name. It is said the sweetest sound in the world is a person's own name.

How many times have you been visiting another city and looked through the telephone book for your own surname? When a photograph is taken of a large group of people, who do you usually look for first? Yourself! The sweetest sound in the world is our own name. Knowing your prospect's name will give you power. (See Chapter 9 on remembering names.)

The acronym "FORT" is something that you should memorize and get with every referral. FORT means:

> **F** amily name
> **O** ccupation
> **R** eligion
> **T** ime they are home.

These four pieces of information will help you make better use of your time and make many more sales. Knowing the family's name will personalize your call. Knowing the children's ages can help determine the books you show. The person's occupation will tell you the hours they work and when is a good time to catch them home. It may also help you to put them at ease as you now can ask intelligent questions about their work and interest. Knowing their occupation will also tell you something about their ability to buy. If you know their religion, it will make quite a difference in the terms to use. For instance, Catholics like to hear "Holy Bible" or "The Gospel of St. John." If they are Bible fundamentalists, you should know special terms they like to hear also. You want to reassure the fundamentalist, "Mr. Jones, we guarantee this to follow the Bible completely, and that's important, isn't it?"

Evangelist John Fowler invited me to help in his evangelistic meetings in Debrecen, Hungary. While there, I met some local literature evangelists. They wanted to know how an American would canvass. I spent much of my time working with them. Three of us went to every door, a translator for me and the literature evangelist of the day I worked with. I did not know the language or the books. I soon found everybody we met was either Catholic or Reformed. My first question was are you Catholic or Reformed? Whatever their answer, I would say, "Wonderful! Then you believe in the Bible." From there I would share with them that we had books that answer man's greatest questions. Where did we come from? Why are we here? What does the Bible say will happen to Hungary in the future? and Does God have a plan for you and this troubled world? As long as we have the *Desire of Ages* and *Great Controversy,* the greatest books written outside the Bible, we can frame questions that will spark interest in any honest soul regardless of their background.

After you've made a sale, it is easy to ask, "Do you know some of your friends or neighbors who would appreciate a service like this?" There are many sales organizations in the world that never spend money on advertising, and their sales people work strictly from referrals.

A literature evangelist was speaking to a lady who was a referral. "How did you get my name?" she asked. The literature evangelist flashed a big smile and said, "Oh good people are well known." She smiled. It is always amazing how when you smile, other people will smile back. Later she purchased books, and she learned how he got her name.

When canvassing, it is always a good idea to have two pens. A literature evangelist without a good pen, is like a bear hunter going hunting with only a little stick. You never know when a pen will run out of ink. You should also always have a note pad. Keep your these in your coat pocket if you are wearing a suit. If you work in a warm climate and do not wear a suit coat, be careful not to put too much in your shirt pocket. Keep some material in your briefcase. A pocket stuffed with items is a sign of a careless and disorganized dresser.

When you call at a home and no one is home it usually means one of two things. They are away making money or spending it. Either way they are good prospects! If you have plenty of leads and referrals, still knock on random doors occasionally. A great deal of information may be gathered as you drive by a house. You see toys in the yard. What does it mean? Usually there are children in the home, and the parents spend money on their children. You may see a sign that says, "No Sales Agents." What does that sign mean? It means "I have poor sales resistance." Such a person is almost always a good prospect. Don't be discouraged by people who have this type of sign, and definitely don't pass them by.

One successful lady literature evangelist in Pennsylvania had a lead card that would have discouraged the faint of heart. On the card was written the following negative messages: "No agents! Don't send agent, no agent, send by mail, no agent, please." All of this was written on the face of this card. Another literature evangelist who originally received this card said, "Oh, I don't want to run this." But this woman said, "Let me have it. I'll be glad to run it." When she arrived at the home and presented the card, the lady exclaimed, "I said no agents!" The optimistic literature evangelist said pleasantly, "Oh, but what I have got to share is so important! I will only take a few minutes of your time." The lady who didn't want any agents, invited her in, and the literature evangelist left with a sale. Another literature evangelist reported a sale at a home where there was a sign on the door, "I shoot every third salesman and the second just left." We are not ordinary salespeople. We are God's ambassadors. There is an old saying that states, "The bearer of good news can knock louder." As one general told his soldiers, "He that storms the fort will have something to report."

2. Action at the Door

When you get out of your car and walk to the door, walk like a person who has purpose and who is on an important errand. You shouldn't take long when you get out of the car. You should shut the car door quietly and walk erectly. You don't want someone to look out the door or window and see a person with a long face and say, "Here comes trouble, I've got enough troubles already." Make it a point to look happy and look like you are glad to be there. One of the publishing leaders in Africa used to say, "These giant vultures here can clean a dead animal in a few hours. When you see them circling above, remember they are watching you. Make sure that they know that you are not dead but alive!" Promptness beats the devil. When you approach the door, be prompt, know exactly where your briefcase is, with every item in place, smile and walk with a triumphant step!

"The canvasser is engaged in an honorable business, and he should not act as though he were ashamed of it. If he would have success attend his efforts, he must be courageous and hopeful." CM, p. 62.

While working in Kazakhstan in the former Soviet Union, I found that some literature evangelists were making their sales at the door. They didn't get into the home, as I was accustomed to doing. However I found that the people would let us in if we expected to get in. Most of us we will not sell much at the door, other than small books. If you want to sell a large set, you need to be in the home, to be able to set the people at ease. One survey in America said that only one person in three hundred will buy a large set of books at the door. If you get in and sit down and talk with the prospect, you should be able to sell one out of three.

There is character in a knock. When you approach the house knock five or six times, starting with a light rap and making it harder with each knock. We don't want to scare the people, but we want them to be sure and hear us. Remember the bearer of good tidings can always knock louder.

Getting past that thin door and into the home depends a great deal upon your action at the threshold. Steve Abbey, who helped train me, told of how he once did the disappearing act. When you knock at the door and the people answer, you should take a step back to disarm them, letting them know that you are not trying to force your way in. Steve said, that unfortunately, he did not measure the distance back to the edge of the rather high porch. When the person came to the door, Steve stepped back and fell off the side of the porch. This disappearing act was not a part of his planned presentation!

When calling on someone who has been referred, we should say, in an upbeat positive tone, "Good morning Mrs. Jones?" Wait for a response before continuing. "I am Bill Beckworth. Mr. and Mrs. Simpson from your church referred me to you. They recommended you as a concerned Christian. May I step in while I explain? Thank you."

What is said at the door is usually better if it's brief and to the point. It's also important to give your name. People want to know who you are—that you are not just some hobo going down the street. Step forward lean and down pick up your briefcase. Your body language says you expect to get in. When I worked in Colorado and Wyoming where there was lots of snow, I would hit my feet together knocking the snow off my shoes, letting the prospect know I expected to come in. It is amazing that when we act positive and expectant, people tend to respond positively. As I have stated earlier, people will often say "You know, I never let strangers in, but you look different." You'd better pray to God that you do look different because people will respond if you do. If you don't get in, do not sit down on the steps and begin crying. Hurry on to the next place. You may be surprised at developments that may bring you back to that house later.

I called back on one of my customers with the hope of showing more books. When she answered the door, I introduced myself and asked her if she remembered me. She said, "Yes, Bill, I enjoyed the books, but I don't need any more." I said, "That's fine,

Mrs. Wainwright." We visited briefly at the door, and then she invited me in. After we renewed our friendship, I asked her, "Mrs. Wainwright, you know, we do have other books. Could I just show you some of the samples?" She said, "Well, okay." After viewing these books, again the Lord touched her heart, and she bought another set. It wasn't long after this that we were able to get studies started in her home. She and her husband joined the church. They have been faithful and active Adventists for 25 years. They would have never become Seventh-day Adventists if I had taken the first "no" at the door. Persistence pays eternal benefits.

Sometimes people say at the door, "Look, I'm so busy." Your response to them is, "I'm busy also. That will help me to be brief" or "My visit will be brief, and if you could allow me five minutes, only your interest will keep me longer." Once you say that, you keep your word and do not take more than that five minutes unless they are interested.

One of the real champions in the literature ministry is Elder Roy Chamberlain. He started canvassing during the great Depression when many ministers didn't have cars. He was one of the first workers to have a car and eventually became a publishing leader and an associate in the Southern Union office. He canvassed a total of 60 years. Many of these years were after he retired. Roy Chamberlain did something that is so important when talking with people. He would look them directly in the eye and nod his head up and down. The old expression, "Monkey see, monkey do" is still true. You should nod your head up and down, smiling and getting the same response from the prospect, as you ask positive questions. You'll find that there is real power in this eye contact and your nod, whether at the door or in your presentation.

Remember that angels attend you, and God wants you to share this message with as many people as possible. Knowing that angels are with us, we have nothing to fear.

3. Expect Success

Expect success at the door as well as in your presentation. If you expect to get in, you will, more often than not. What you say, says you expect to get in. Give God a chance and be positive and expectant. "According to your faith, be it unto you." Matthew 9:29. Behind every door, there is a need. There's a problem and you have books to help with the needs and problems. There is a little poem that states:

Some doors swing, and some doors roll.
Some doors push, and some doors pull.
Some doors sag, with looks of gloom.
Some are stiff as a brand new broom.
But if it moves, with groan or whine,
Or if it swings with welcome fine,
Some soul is there, some soul to win.
The word of God, just must get in.
—Author unknown

4. Getting in Step With the People

If you're going to catch a moving bus you step in the direction the bus is traveling. The same is true with people. If they are moving in a certain direction, move with them. Do not argue with them or go head-on with some idea that they may present. Approach them at an oblique angle. Try finding something for which you can pay them a sincere compliment.

I called on a rural family who had sent in a card asking about our material. When I got to the home, the man came to the door and told me that he didn't like salespeople and that they were not interested. I told him that I traveled a long way out in the country to see him and could he take just a few minutes. Again he assured me that neither he nor his wife liked talking to salespeople. I just backed away a few steps and began talking casually. I heard someone in the background playing a guitar. I began talking about the music that was being played. I asked the man if he were a country music fan, and although I don't know much about music (if you have heard me sing, you'll know that!), we soon had a conversation going. His guard was coming down the more we talked. After he warmed up, I asked again, "Mr. Henderson, I've come a long way. Let me just take a few minutes and share this material with you and your wife. He said, "Well okay, come on in."

Once I was in the home, his wife seemed as obstinate as he had been earlier. Perhaps something had happened in the home just before I arrived or maybe there had been a bad experience with a salesperson in the past. After a little persuasion, the woman sat down beside her husband although she acted agitated as she joined us. An amazing thing happened as I began presenting my books. As I talked about the second coming, and showed them the picture of Jesus coming, telling them how wonderful it will

be sharing that with our families, a change came over this couple.
They became tremendously impressed and began taking the books
out of my hands and looking at them.

Eventually the man said to me, "You know, I've been looking
for two books that my mother used to read to us. She used those
books until she wore the covers off. We lived far out in the country
and seldom ever got to go to a church. Those books were so interesting. One was called *The Great Controversy* and the other was *The
Desire of Ages*." I happily informed him that those two books would
come with this set of children's books. After they purchased, I had
prayer with them, I looked up and both of them had tears in their
eyes. I had just prayed for their children. Maybe they had suffered some tragedy with their children. I do not know the circumstances, but my exit was so different from my entry to that home.
The Holy Spirit had really taken over that presentation. That is
the only thing that could have changed them so much. It really
was not what I said but the Lord using the words that I spoke. As
I left, the man picked up my briefcase and carried it to the car.
They both stood beside my car as I drove away, waving goodbye to
me. By God's blessing, I was able to get in step with those people.

5. Point Out The Need

"In many cases when the canvasser makes known his business,
the door of the heart (or mind) closes firmly; hence, the great
need of doing his work with tact and in humble, prayerful spirit."
CM, p. 63. You must be tactful but point out the need. Use your
prospectus to illustrate the signs of the times, the challenges of
television, divorce and drugs and how these affect the family. You
may want to carry a local newspaper article to point out the need
by some great headline that has made the news in your city. At
least read the paper and be aware of current events.

One study has stated that 75 percent of what people remember
is what they get through the sense of sight and 15 percent from
hearing. Let us combine hearing and sight, then we can make
the greatest possible impact. People already know the need, but
when you point it out, it reinforces what they already know and
helps bring conviction to their heart.

As you show parts of your book always point with a pen, not
your finger. Point with your pen to what you're reading or to the
picture, you want them to look at. The point of your pen is like a
magnet, and their eyes will follow your pen.

6. Visual Aids

Visual aids are vital. Any good instructor has some kind of visual aids. Remember, you want to do all that you can to help the people to realize their big need. Display your books and spread them out so they can see how big they are and how many you have. Dale Carnegie's sales course emphasizes showmanship. Someone has said that there are 300,000 things that anyone can buy. We don't want people to think of this as just one of 300,000 things. But this is the one very special item that they need. Remind the mother as you spread out all of your books, "Mothers of today have the biggest job in the world, but we have the very best tools in the world to help you."

Now the man whom we looked at a little while ago was fearful, preoccupied, and didn't need anything. Suddenly, this man is aware of his need. He likes you. He senses his need and you have not yet shown him all of your books. He is already one-half sold.

Chapter 6

"Declare ye among the nations; and publish, and set up a standard: publish, and conceal not . . .."
Jeremiah 50:2, KJV.

The Presentation

When you present your books, you will not have an announcer and you will not hear applause. But you must be convicted that someone is with you and someone sent you. You realize you are there to help people with a very real need.

I once heard a speaker say, "Good luck is when preparation meets opportunity, and bad luck is when lack of preparation meets opportunity." In other words, if the opportunity presents itself and if you aren't prepared then it is just plain bad luck!!! Your presentation should be prepared. In that 17 to 20 minutes that you make your presentation, what you say determines if you make a sale or not. But more important, it may decide the destiny of the soul.

Good luck is when preparation meets opportunity

I am not sure where I found the following, but it describes Christian salesmanship and our mission. "Salesmanship is the science of creating in the prospect's mind a desire or a want that only the possession of your product will satisfy." When you have

made that want urgent enough, a positive decision will follow with
a decision. Remember, people do not buy what they need, they
buy what they want. It is up to you to help them want what they
truly need. God has given us a special mission. An old adage says,
"You can lead a horse to water but you cannot make the horse
drink." It is not our job to make the horse drink. It is our job to
give the horse salt and make him thirsty!

In the fourth century B.C., the Greek philosopher Aristotle,
said that people are influenced by three things: They're influenced
by ethos, pathos and logic. Each of these are important in your
presentation.

Ethos

Ethos is what people think of you personally. They may like
you. Are you friendly? Are you informed? Are you courteous? An
honest appearing man is more readily believed. Do they sense
that you are sincerely interested in them? The world will listen
to those who are masters of their work.

Pathos

Pathos is that which reaches and raises the emotions: pity,
sorrow, love, fear, pride. Some people will purchase material because of pride. Their neighbor purchased or they want it on their
bookshelf. Some people purchase for fear of family members being eternally lost. They may purchase because they love their
children and they want the very best material to help them. The
loss of a loved one or sorrow may cause someone to feel the need.
Someone may be concerned for a less fortunate family member
who needs your material. Some people have a deep love for their
Maker and want to understand the Bible better. Some may see
no need in their own lives, but have a burden for their grandchildren. These are all buying motives.

In *The Bible Story,* volume nine, page 118-123, "Goodby Mother,"
is truly a heart-touching story that appeals to pathos. More than
once, I have looked up from reading the last portion of this story
and have seen tears coming from someone's eyes. Pathos brings
conviction. The mother's love is a powerful pathos that will help
move people to a decision.

Bob Lee, a literature evangelist from the Colorado Conference
shared with me the following story. One of his customers told
how her husband had a beer every evening as he sat watching

television. The little girl read the chapter in *Your Bible and You on* "Unwise Drinking." She brought this into her father showing it to him and said, "Daddy, do you know what the Bible says about drinking?" The father looked down at his little girl and said, "Honey, I never knew it meant so much to you." He went to the sink and poured the beer into the sink. The little girl said, "Daddy, you have more in the refrigerator." He went to the refrigerator and poured the rest into the sink. The mother told our literature evangelist, "Those books have been worth much more than the money that we spent on them." Stories like this can be used in your presentation where applicable. They add pathos or emotion that touch the heart. This moves people to make the logical decision they know they should make.

I heard a story about a little girl who came home from school and said, "Mama, today I fell and hurt myself. I cut my knee, and Jane helped me more than anybody." Mother asked, "Well, honey, what did Jane do?" The little girl responded," Well, when I cried, Jane cried." That is powerful pathos.

Remember laughter is an emotion also. If you and the prospect laugh during first five minutes of the call, the likelihood of closing the sale dramatically increases. Dale Carnegie wisely observed, "When dealing with people, remember you are not dealing with creatures of logic, but creatures of emotion." What feels more emotionally delightful and satisfying than a simultaneous laugh with someone? A laugh quickly advances the relationship past the initial introduction and into a more personal realm.

Logic

Logic will tell people what they ought to do. You must have the ethos. You must appeal to the pathos, but you must have solid logic to support what you say.

The following are the steps to a good presentation:

1. Get the Family Together

It is very difficult to sell a husband if the wife is not sitting beside him where both can see and appreciate the benefits of your presentation. It is best to get every member of the family together before making a presentation. There are exceptions to this, but generally we should have the family together. If a family member that enters the room during the middle of your presentation or sits too far away, they will not understand all the benefits.

This individual is usually the one who will kill the sale. If grandmother or any visiting relative is there, have them sit down. You are always better off if you have everyone in the house sitting and listening to your canvass.

What if the husband comes home in the middle of your presentation? The first thing you should do is (smile), jump to your feet, go over and look him in the eye, extend your hand, and say, "Mr. Jones, I'm so glad you got here. I'm just sharing this wonderful children's literature with your wife. I want to show you also. Would you mind sitting beside her while I continue?" Then start from the beginning of the presentation and go through it again. You want him to know everything that she knows. When an intruder comes in during the middle of your presentation, always greet the newcomer pleasantly even though you know it is not the best way to make a presentation.

Elder Ted Smith, the Associate Publishing Director of the Southern Union, shared an incident where he could not get the family together. He called at the home of a lady, not knowing that she was a spiritualist medium. It was a hot summer day. She did not have air conditioning, so he made his presentation on her front porch. He heard a noise, looked up and saw a figure behind the screen door. He stood to ask this person to join them in his presentation. As he asked the individual to come out and join them, the lady said, "Oh don't mind him. That's my father. He's been dead for ten years." Elder Smith thought he had misunderstood and asked her to repeat what she said. She said the same thing again. He sat back down and began his presentation again when he heard pots and pans banging around in the kitchen. The lady said, "Please excuse me. I've got to fix my father's lunch." Ted told her he had to go also! He said to me with a chuckle, "Bill, that is one time I did not try to get the whole family to sit together!"

2. Display Your Books Well

Remember people learn 75 percent from the sense of sight, the rest from feeling and hearing. Make sure the light is shining favorably on your books so they can be shown to the best advantage. Hold the books so the prospect can see the writing. As you point out your favorite lines which you have memorized, point with your pen so the customer can follow easily as you read. By memorizing lines you can hold the book up-side and read as the prospect follows. Make sure that they can see where you are pointing. The point is like a magnet, and their eyes will follow your pen. Always use your pen, not your finger, to point with. While you do not want to sit too close to prospects, you should be able to get on one knee or be close enough that they can see your books. Never sit so close, though, that you make the person feel uncomfortable.

It is best not to let the prospect take the book from your hand until you are ready to begin the close. If she is looking at a book and you are trying to show another book, you will not have her full attention. When starting your close, allow the prospect to hold and feel the book. Of course, if in the middle of your presentation, someone takes the book and holds it close and says, "I love these books, I want them," don't feel that you must make the rest of your presentation. As one literature evangelist said, "But lady, you can't purchase these yet. I haven't given you all of my presentation!" If they are ready to buy at that point, go ahead and write up the order.

3. Speak Clearly

Your family and your associates may understand when you speak. But as you start the canvassing work, you must be certain to enunciate your words clearly. Say them in a distinct manner that will be understood by the prospect. As Ellen White counseled, "In full round tones" CM, p. 71. I've heard literature evangelists say that they would stand and read their books aloud for 15 minutes, working on their diction. Others have said they would sit erect and read their books. I promise you this, if you will read from the Bible and from your books aloud for fifteen minutes each day, you will be amazed at how it will help your speaking ability. Always pause at punctuation marks. Do not let your voice drop off at the end of a sentence. Emphasize key words. A good voice commands attention. "Never search for words that will give the impression that you are learned. The greater your simplicity, the better will your words be understood" *Ibid*. Read aloud or speak into a tape recorder or video camera and play it back. Don't be discouraged when you first hear your voice recorded, but continue practicing, and you will see improvement. Ask someone else, such as your publishing leader or your church pastor, to listen and make suggestions. Good speech is more precious than gold. Words are fingers that mold the minds of men.

Read the following quotation graphically and with enthusiasm.

See how words paint pictures: "A marred 78-year-old fireball pro-
pelled by a cane and followed by a little nervous female shadow,
stormed into the optometrist office. He thrust his face into the
face of the doctor's assistant and sputtered with rage, 'Look at
my nose. Just look at what these glasses of yours have done to
my nose!' " Can you see the picture?

Ellen White, although she never went to college or took a course
in public speaking, developed by God's blessing, into an outstand-
ing speaker. Without the aid of a public address system she could
address thousands of people and be heard and understood distinctly.

"On a certain occasion, when Betterton, the celebrated actor,
was dining with Dr. Sheldon, Archbishop of Canterbury, the Archbishop said to him, 'Pray, Mr. Betterton, tell me why it is that you
actors affect your audiences so powerfully by speaking of things
imaginary.' 'My lord,' replied Betterton, 'with due submission to
Your Grace, permit me to say that the reason is plain; it all lies in
the power of enthusiasm. We on the stage speak of things imaginary as if they were real; and you in the pulpit speak of things
real as if they were imaginary.' " EV, p. 179.

Remember, also, what was said earlier, that prayer does wonders for our presentation. "It [prayer] will give to the voice a persuasive power." MH, p. 512.

4. Enthusiasm

"Talk and act as if your face is invincible." CM, p. 18. If you
practice this, you will become enthusiastic. Someone described
enthusiasm as conviction set on fire. Enthusiasm comes from the
Greek word which means "God within." One sales book states
that, "Any salesman who is not fired with enthusiasm should be
fired with enthusiasm." If you're going to be successful, you must
be enthusiastic. Emerson, the early American philosopher, said,
"The difference between a man and a statue is enthusiasm." Notice the sequence of the statement in *Colporteur Ministry*, "Talk
and act as if." Act as if your faith is invincible, and it will be. We
gain faith as we take action. The same is true of enthusiasm or
any other character trait you want. William James, called the
father of modern psychology, spent 15 years at Harvard University studying human motivation. His summation of that study
was that people can have any character trait they want if they
will "act as if" they have it. He also said "People don't sing be-

cause they are happy, but they are happy because they sing." Act enthusiastic, and eventually enthusiasm or whatever trait you are working on will become part of you. This does not mean you should be bouncing off walls. People who bounce off walls usually go as low as they get high. Being continually enthusiastic and upbeat can be you, if you choose to be. Everyone likes to work with this type of person, and customers like to do business with people who believe in what they are doing.

> **Talk and act as if you are enthusiastic, and soon you will be.**

I have heard retired publishing leader, Bill Miller, tell many times of the power of enthusiasm that career literature evangelist, Harvey Yawn, used in selling. Once Harvey went to call on a lead several miles from home and found he had forgotten the book that the prospect had asked for, *Bible Reading for the Home*. Harvey was not going to let this keep him from making a presentation. After all, he had a little picture of it on the lead card. He knocked on the lady's door, showed her the card, and she invited him in. All he had was an order pad and the card. He told the women that he had forgotten the book, but that he could tell about it. He gave a brief presentation and said, "Ma'am, the book is about this tall, it's about this wide, and it's about this thick." (He said this with great enthusiasm.) "And you are going to love this book. It is only $_____. You'll have your book in two weeks." The lady said, "I'll take it." She said, "You know, I think my sister who lives just down the road would also like a book like that." Harvey, fired with even more enthusiasm went down to see her sister. He told her a few facts about the book and said with enthusiasm, "The book is about this tall, it's about this wide, and it's about this thick. Your sister got one of these, and she is excited about it, and I know you are going to be too! This will be such a blessing to you as you study your Bible! This book is only . . ." He asked for the order and got it. All these ladies saw was a little picture on a card, and they both ordered the book! It was not the facts that Harvey shared that convinced them to buy the book. It was his enthusiasm and belief in what he was doing. This is not a recommended method, but it does show the power of enthusiasm.

> "In proportion to the enthusiasm and perseverance with which the work is carried forward, will be the success given."—Patriarchs and Prophets, pp. 263, 264

5. Ask Questions

This is the most powerful thing that you can learn in your Christian salesmanship. This is a skill that can be learned and it is the most useful tool in communication. Ask the right questions, and you get the right answers. You must have the right questions throughout your presentation as you come to the close.

Jesus often answered questions with questions. Jesus was the greatest salesman who ever lived. If someone asks you, "What happens when a man dies?" You know, and you may be full of quotations that will answer the question, but it is much better for you to leave a book in that home that will answer the question over and over and over and give the family a complete Bible study. So instead of answering the question, say this: "You know, Mr. Jones, that's an interesting question. Why do you ask?"

Here is one of the most difficult things for some people to master. But it is what makes a person a great conversationalist and a great salesperson. When you make a query, do not answer it for the person! You may want to respond or you may feel your question made them a little uneasy. After you ask the question, be quiet. Listen to what they have to say. Often they will tell you a great story—sometimes a story that will help you close other sales as well. What you want to know is: What is in that person's mind? What is he or she thinking? Why does he ask this question? It may be altogether a different reason from what you are thinking. By asking questions, you draw thoughts out from your prospect and make your pathway toward the close of the sale so much easier because you can refer back to his statement. This will be covered in more detail in the chapter, "Answering Objections," page 85. When you ask a question, it makes the person curious and helps you keep his attention. If you answer all the questions that he has, there is no need for him to purchase your material.

Dale Carnegie says, "A man convinced against his will is of the same opinion still." We do not build a sale on disagreements, we build it on agreements. Ask questions and build a bridge to the prospect's island. What he says to you will help you build that bridge to his special island and help him to know that your books have the answers that he needs. Someone may say to you, "Are you Jehovah's Witness?" I once worked with a literature evangelist who would always answer, "Oh absolutely not." We were in a home, and the customer was interested in our health books. She asked the literature evangelist, "Are you Jehovah's Witness?" The literature evangelist gave his trademark answer, "Absolutely not." Generally, that's a good answer. Unless of course you're talking to a Jehovah's Witness. The lady said, "Well I am." Obviously, her interest died at that point. It's much better to answer that question this way, "Why do you ask? Are you a Jehovah's Witness?" If someone says, "Are you a Seventh-day Adventist?" Answer them saying, "Why? Are you Seventh-day Adventist?" You may think they are prejudiced against Adventism. In fact, they may be very favorable toward it. By answering with a question and a smile, you can find out what they are thinking. If a prospect asks a question, and you're not sure where he/she is going, you can answer, "What do you have in mind?"

6. Third Party Selling

We use a story of a third party when answering objections and also in our presentation. Mention a visit to the home of someone with whom you think the prospect may identify. You can tell how a third person used these books to help their children. For example, I related what one customer told me. She said, "My son had nightmares until we stopped his watching TV just before he went to bed. Instead we read these books to him." Now the prospect can see herself in this third person's experience. But if you had said to her, "Your child would sleep better if you would turn off the TV and read to her each night from these books," you would seem to be preachy and talking down to the prospect. An altogether different approach, but the same thing was said.

Third person selling can be effective in your presentation. When I'm in a home where people already have several books, I tell about a doctor that I called on who said to me, "You know Bill, I already have those books." He pointed to a wall of book shelves. "I have all of these books, but *The Bible Story* books are the most used books in my home." Your publishing leader and fellow literature evangelists will have many stories like this to share with you, and you will build your own as you canvass. You can also use personal testimonials of how the books have been a blessing to you. You may even want to carry a written testimonial from one of your customers.

Sometimes we get wonderful letters, not only from parents but from elderly people. An 80 year old wrote, "I've learned more in the last three months reading these children's books than I have learned by going to church the last 30 years."

7. Give An Example

Give an example of how to use the books—particularly the index. This is especially important with the health books. Give testimonials of how they have saved someone's life. Tell how these books helped someone treat their family at home and saved the expense of an office call. There are so many things we can do at home.

To a weary mother, read from the *Desire of Ages,* page 461, "Jesus knows the burden of every mother's heart." This is a powerful paragraph and lets the mother see how these books will bring a blessing to her. Another great quote when people say, "Does God really care? I don't think God really understands all of my problems," is *Desire of Ages*, page 434: "God know us individually. He knows the very house we live in; H e knows all the people in the house." Then look the person in the eyes and say, "Mrs. Jones, personally, I have found a great deal of comfort from reading this book and I know it will bring you the same blessing." *Colporteur Ministry*, page 85 states, "You cannot regard them [our books] too highly."

8. Keep Your Presentation Spiritual

There is not another salesperson who will have the spiritual approach that you can have. Keep your presentation Christ-centered and the Lord will bless. When you speak of the Lord in loving terms, angels will draw near and the Holy Spirit will come in to speak with the people. Remember the promise that angels do travel with you. On more than one occasion, people have seen another person walking beside the literature evangelist and that person is surely an angel

Richard Basini was a career literature evangelist in Swaziland. He told me that every day he would start his day by going out into the banana groves early in the morning to pray and have Bible study. His neighbor lived on a hill above him. One day his neighbor ask him, "Mr. Basini what do you every morning for so long in the banana groves. Brother Basini answered, "Oh that is when I go for prayer and Bible study." His neighbor replied, "But who is it that goes with you each day?" "Oh, no one. I go by myself." "But I see another man go with you, and he is always dressed in white." Bother Basini said, "Then you must have seen my angel!"

In your presentation, use the name of Jesus often. "No sooner is the name of Jesus mentioned in love and tenderness, than the angels of God draw near to soften and subdue the heart." CM, p. 112. That is the most powerful tool that we have. This quote has been most precious to me through the years. We have this special power that people selling ordinary products can't claim. As I wrote this page, I got a call from a customer who said of Tim Merryman, a literature evangelist in Chattanooga, Tennessee, "I just called to let you know that your sales representative is one of the nicest people that I have ever met. He really represents your company well. I've never met anybody quite like him." Tim had given a spiritual presentation, and it had touched her heart.

> **"No sooner is the name of Jesus mentioned in love and tenderness, than angels draw near to soften and subdue the heart."** *Colporteur Ministry,* **p. 112.**

"The Savior knew that no argument, however logical, would melt hearts or break through the crust of worldliness and selfishness. He knew His disciples must receive the heavenly endowment, that the gospel would be effective only as it was proclaimed by hearts made warm and lips made eloquent by living knowledge of Him who is the Way, the Truth and the Light." AP, p. 33.

9. Show The People How To Use Your Books

I canvassed a lady in north Florida who said she was in a hurry that evening. I made my presentation and wasn't sure if she were seeing the benefits of these books as I went through my canvass. At the beginning of my presentation I had asked her, "Why did you send in the card?" She told me that she was a Sunday School teacher. She was not interested for her own family, but for Sunday School. As I neared the close of the sale, I said to her, "You know Mrs. Johnson, when you come in on Saturday night and you have had a busy week and maybe you have not had the time you need to prepare for Sunday School, you have 411 stories in this index and you can quickly find one that fits your needs. Here you have all the Bible men and women listed alphabetically, and your Sunday School lessons usually involve some character in the Bible, don't they?" She agreed. "Do you see how this can be a help to you in teaching your Sunday School class? I looked her in the eye as I asked this question. She looked at me and said, "I hear you talking." I knew that she was thinking now of purchasing the material and all I had to do now was ask the right closing questions. She did buy, not only the children's material but all the adult books also. As I left that home, I thanked the Lord that He impressed me to ask the questions I did in the beginning. It enabled me to show this women what she was most interested in. She now teaches with these every week.

If your presentation follows the guidelines in this chapter, your close will be easy. The man we looked at earlier has changed his mind about your product. Now with a smooth close that makes it easy for him to say "yes," he will have your truth filled books in his home.

Chapter 7

*". . . Not by might, nor by power,
but by my spirit, saith the Lord of Hosts."*
Zechariah 4:6, KJV.

The Close

I f God be for us, who can be against us?" Romans 8:31. One little girl put it another way, when asked to quote this as a memory verse, "If God is not for you, then you are up against it." When you come to the close, you need confidence. And why shouldn't you be confident? This is the reason that you came, to close the sale, and leave this wonderful material with the people. But if you are going to close right, you must start right. The close or action part of the sale as it may be called, really started when you first knocked on the door. But it is a very important step of the sale. Knowing how to ask the people to buy is often the key to whether you'll make a sale or not. Now we are going to look at ways to make closing the sale easier.

1. Review Your Main Points

It is easy for people to forget what you've said in your enthusiastic presentation. You should have had four or five key points in your presentation. As you come to the end and ask for the order, review each of these points very briefly. Take no more than thirty seconds. You want your main selling benefits fixed in their mind again just before you ask for the order.

71

Remember as you summarize to nod your head again up and down, looking them in the eye. The old adage is true, "Monkey see, monkey do." You nod your head, and they will nod their head in agreement. It is so much easier if their head is going up and down when they reach for their checkbook than if it is going in a negative mode, left to right. If they agree throughout your presentation and during your close, it's not difficult to get them to agree when it is time to write the deposit or full amount at the end of your presentation.

2. Exalt The Value

When people raise objections—and you should expect them—respond briefly. Don't spend a lot of time. Use some reserve points and move on. To exalt the value, we compare our product to another set of books, such as the encyclopedia which costs many times more. If it's a single volume, compare it to love stories, novels, mysteries or just ordinary books that are not true and don't really help the family at all. Our book builds character and prepares people for heaven. Often, quality books sold in the store will be more than our single volume.

"God calls upon His people to act like living men and not to be indolent, sluggish and indifferent. We must carry the publications to the people and URGE them to accept, showing them that they will receive more than their money's worth. EXALT THE VALUE of the books you offer. You cannot regard them too high." CM, p. 85. The emphases have been added here to the words EXALT and URGE. If we realize the importance of our calling, we would truly EXALT the value and URGE people to buy. There is a soul weighing in the balance.

Some may say, "That sounds like you're pressuring people." I don't like using that word because I don't want the people to feel any pressure. One man said to me as I was closing a sale, "Don't pressure me." I said, "You know, Mr. Towson, the only pressure I want you to feel is that of the Holy Spirit telling you what to do." We want to let the Lord help us in this, but when Jesus comes, people will be glad that we **URGED** them to buy. Throughout eternity, people will be thankful that we gave them a sanctified nudge to make the right decision. Is it possible to exalt the value of our books too high?

The Bible uses some pretty strong language concerning our commission. "And the Lord said unto the servant, Go out into the highways and hedges, and compel them to come in that my house may be filled." Luke 14:23. Compel them to come in! Our mission is important. Our literature has eternal value!

> **"We must carry the publications to the people and urge them to accept, showing them that they will get more than their money's worth. Exalt the value of the books you offer"** CM. p. 85.

At this point, someone will say, "I'll bet you would take someone's last dollar if that's all they had to purchase your books, wouldn't you?" My response is, "Absolutely!" We just read from the pen of inspiration, "You cannot regard them too highly." Remember the story of Elijah and the widow—how God blessed her when she used her last bread to feed Elijah. Eternity is in the balance. God will provide. Furthermore, we have literature of every price, and often we give away small books.

Larry Cansler, a literature evangelist in Missouri, shared this story with me. A lady told him that all the money she had in the house was the money that she was going to use to buy food for her family the next day. Larry hesitated and told her that he didn't really want to take her last money, but the lady insisted and reminded Larry of the promises he had just given her, such as "Seek ye first the kingdom of God and His righteousness and all these things will be added unto you." Matthew 6:33. "You do believe this, don't you?" Larry reassured her that he did. She took her last money and made a down payment on the books. Larry went by to see this lady a month later. The lady laughed when she came to the door. She said, "I guess you came by to see if we were starving. Well, the next day we got some money unexpectedly that was enough to make up for what I paid down on those books." God still works, and He blesses those who sacrifice for the right reasons.

Let me digress and tell of how God's blessed my wife and me. We lived in Johannesburg, South Africa and we were down to our last 40 rand. We could purchase all of our favorite foods in that city if we had the money. Duane McKee brought down a truck from Zaire to get supplies for the missionaries in Zaire and Zambia. We had close friends at two of these stops. Dale and Joy Tho-

mas, in Lusaka, Zambia and Leif and Donna Hansen in Lubum-
basi, Zaire. We knew they couldn't get the nice peanut butter and
fresh apples we could. We packed food for each family spending
our last 40 rand. Forty rand at that time was equal to almost 50
US dollars. The truck pulled out for the North on Sunday and on
Monday we got a letter from an old friend back in Kansas. In
that letter was a check for 50 US dollars! Amazing? Yes! You see
this lady was a member of the Baptist church of which we were
once members. She said that she was just thinking of us and
wanted to help in our work in Africa. Can God provide when we
do what is right? Absolutely!

Exalt the value of your books and minimize the cost. Then
urge them to make a decision. If you sell a $700 set, make sure
you give a $2,000 presentation. You exalt the value of your books
by comparing your set to another product that people may purchase—such as some electronic gadget which may cost $2,000
and doesn't do anything for the family's spirituality. One man
told us that he bought a television dish which only brought the
devil into his home, and he had spent $4,000 for it. He said, "You
know, these books are what I've needed and what my children
need, not 35 channels on the television. If this would just save
one of my children from getting involved in an abusive relationship or to avoid the temptation of drugs, it would be worth many
times what I'm spending on them." He exalted the value for the
literature evangelist. He also minimized the cost. Memorize this
story and use it.

In communication it makes a difference what words you emphasize in your presentation. For instance, I once watched the
presentation of a man selling vacuum sweepers, and he had all
kinds of gadgets spread across the floor. He spread his arms out
in an exaggerated way, and said you get all-l-l-l-l of this for only
$950. He emphasized "all" and "only." His voice lowered when
he said the actual amount. He was exalting the value and mini-
mizing the cost. He emphasized the points that he wanted remembered in his close. Little words, such as, "all," "big" and
"only" are powerful words and paint the important benefits.
Little words help people make big decisions. Everywhere I've
gone, I have asked the literature evangelists in training schools
to emphasize "only" in their language. In southern Africa we
had many languages and each one had a very different word for
"only": in Zulu, it is *kuphella*, in Xhosa, *qha*, in Sotho, *fella*.

There is an equivalent word in every language, and its use is important.

As I finished a presentation the lady said, "I'm interested in your *Bible Story Books* but I already have *Bible Readings*." I said, "Oh that's wonderful. Have you enjoyed it?" This could have been a dangerous question, but I read from her expression that she had a positive experience with this book. Her answer set the stage for the next purchase she was going to make from me. She said, "Yes I love that book, *Bible Readings*. I use it a lot. If I had to get rid of all of my books and could only keep one, it would be *Bible Readings*." When I tell this story I raise my voice slightly and emphasize "could only keep one."

I called on a Catholic school, and the principal was a nun who had purchased a set of our books before. She purchased another set and said to me, "You know every Catholic home should have a set of these." You can be sure that whenever I am in a Catholic home, I quote that nun, and I have for twenty-five years. You can use this story also. Again, as you tell the story, emphasize in "every Catholic home."

When someone convinces you that he can't afford to buy the books and you leave without a sale, if the home seems to have the appearance of affluence and if you see a $20,000 car in the driveway, who sold whom? In the story of Elijah, he sold the woman. The woman believed, and the woman was blessed. One literature evangelist tells the story of how he came to a home where he had an appointment. The lady told him how she was looking forward to getting these books. She said she had gone to the bank that day for the money to make sure she had enough. She said, "I drew out $1,000." How much were these books worth to her? Much more than what she actually paid! There are many people in the world who appreciate our books much more than our own church members.

3. Coast Past Price

Jesus says, "Be ye therefore wise as serpents and as harmless as doves." Matthew 10:16. Try not to talk too much about the price. When you come to the price, don't emphasize it, but coast past the price. Make it easy for them to buy. Don't let them see a dollar sign when they look into your eyes. "These are only $700." Lower your voice as you get to the price. "Mrs. Jones, in this *Bible Reference Library* series, there are 3,992 scripture references, one of the finest commentaries that you can get. In *Bible Reading*, there are over 4,000 Bible questions answered. All of this is only $500. Or all of this is only $—— down and $—— each month. At this point of the sale, some literature evangelists get nervous and are afraid to show the price. Don't be afraid. Think big. Show a large unit. Remember, when you show a large unit, you can always back off to a smaller one. But vice versa is difficult.

4. Use A Minor Point

This is crucial in closing the sale smoothly. Never ask the customer, "Do you want these?" The customer will seldom respond in a positive way to a question like that. Ask them a question that is easy to answer. Lead them step by step. I've closed many sales without the customer ever saying, "I want the books," but they continue answering minor points.

This principle is used by any pastor who is a successful soul winner. I'll never forget watching Pastor David Rose, who was my pastor in Casper, Wyoming. My mother was visiting from Texas and was only with us a few days. I asked the pastor if he would visit with my mother, as I found it hard to ask her if she were ready to join the Adventist Church. I knew my mother had read every issue of *Signs of the Times* and she had read *Desire of Ages* through three times. She seemed in agreement with our beliefs.

Pastor Rose came to our home, sat with my mother and asked her what she thought of each major doctrinal point of the Adventist church. She had a question in four areas. Each evening he came and gave her a Bible study. At the end of the fourth day, he asked if she agreed with the point studied that day. As after each study, her answer was "yes." Pastor Rose saw her as a candidate for the conference church. After the fourth study, he knew she understood this message. He had a paper with the statement of our beliefs, including the points that they had studied together. He never asked, "Do you want to join the Adventist church?" She had already been baptized by immersion and had accepted the Lord as her Savior many years before. He handed her a document and said, "Mrs. Beckworth, you agree with all of this. Just sign right here." My wife and I looked on in disbelief. We felt that my mother had not understood what she had just done. As soon as he left, my wife turned to my mother and said, "Mother, do you understand what you've just done?" Her response was, "Well, yes, I just joined the Seventh-day Adventist Church." From then on she paid tithe. She was never able to belong to local church, but her commitment was made to the church by such a simple method of closing. The pastor received agreement on minor points and assumed the positive conclusion. A step in faith was made because of this technique. Any literature evangelist who wants to be successful must learn to master the technique of using minor points and assuming the positive.

Never say to a prospect, "Do you want to buy this set of books?" Instead say, "If you were to get these today, how would you take care of this, on an easy payment plan or would you take care of it all at once with a check?" Remember when you ask a closing question, this is a critical point. Please don't say another word. You must listen to what the customer says. Possibly, she is not ready to buy yet and needs to hear another benefit. The prospect will let you know what she is thinking, if you ask the right question and remain quiet and listen. Remain quiet even if she does not say anything. A few seconds of being quiet may seem like hours to you, but usually it is only a matter of seconds. When the prospect say's, "Oh, I will get them on the easy payment plan," then ask another easy question. "What is today's date?" You know the date, but you want her to tell you the date because when you write it on the contract, she knows you are writing it on the contract. Every time she answers another question, she is saying, "Yes, I want these books." Your next question would be, "What is your zip code?" Then, "Let's see now, your address is . . ." You know the answer to each question, but you want the prospect to answer. By doing this you are making it easy for her to buy. Many people will buy, but never say, "Yes I want these." They want you to help them in their decision.

One elderly lady looked at me and said laughingly, "You act like you really think I'm going to purchase these." If I had told her at that point, "Oh no!" I probably would not have made the sale. She was testing me. Smiling back I answered her, as I nodded my head up and down, "Ma'am, you do need these, don't you?" (It's incredulous in my mind that she could possibly think otherwise!) In closing the sale always keep it spiritual. This is a serious time when we want the Holy Spirit to lead.

Most folks make major decisions on minor points. People will buy a house because of a small feature one house has over another.

This is true in all kind of sales. Salespeople ask for a decision on minor items moving the prospect toward the bigger decision and signing a contract. We move people toward an eternal decision.

Annalisa Helavera of Finland was for years the world's champion literature evangelist. She specialized in putting more than one set of books in the home. Especially when she called on grandparents, she would ask the question, "Now, do you want a set for each of your grandchildren or just one set for your home?" The power of suggestion is wonderful and many times she sold more than one set in the home. Sometimes she would say, "You have three children. When they grow up, they will have families of their own and each will want a set of these books. Do you want a set for each of your children?" She said it was amazing, how many times at her suggestion, parents would purchase a set of books for each of their children. A major decision made on a minor point.

5. Close One At A time

Occasionally circumstances may force you to have more than one family viewing your presentation at one time. This usually is not good. Often people are afraid to commit in front of a friend, while if you had each family alone they would have followed their convictions and purchased. It is almost always better to see one interested family at a time. The same is true when giving Bible studies. Large numbers may be baptized in an evangelistic series, but generally the decision was made by each individual home alone with a Bible worker or pastor.

When you have more than one family, concentrate on the interest you came to see first. Get a closure on that individual or family and then turn to other interested parties. Many sales have been lost because the canvasser became anxious and jumped from one interest to another. The first interest's decision has a big influence on the second or third interest, especially if it is negative.

6. Talk Success

"Talk and act as if your faith is invincible." CM, p. 115. My faith is not always invincible. But I try never to reveal it by talking negatively. Satan can not read your thoughts, and you don't want to encourage him. God will bless those who talk and act positively. Positive speech goes against humanity's sinful negative inclination. The devil knows this and is looking for a chink in your armor. Your positive attitude will often react on the customer. I was training a literature evangelist in Wyoming, and it was his very first presentation. As he came to the close, he said to the lady, "Well ma'am, I guess you'll have to talk with your husband before you make a decision on this, won't you?" She laughed and looked at him, "No, isn't that awful?" She laughed again, went to the bedroom and brought back her checkbook and wrote a check for the books. It was his first presentation, and he was nervous, but God overruled his inexperience, and she bought the books in spite of his negative suggestion. Always be positive. We do not know what other people are thinking. They are much more likely to be positive if we are.

7. Use Testimonials

By testimonials, I mean testimonies of how other people have paid for books; stories other literature evangelists will share with you; how others have decided to get these books in spite of being short of money. Bob Merrills, of Chattanooga, Tennessee, likes to tell the story of when he called at a home where the children had been saving for a pony. But as they looked at the books, they told their mother, "Use the money we have been saving for the pony. We'd rather have these books." The mother had to be reassured by the children that it was really their decision. The Lord impressed their little hearts.

8. Reassure Them

Many people who buy our product or any other product, may get what is called buyer's remorse after the purchase. They'll begin thinking, "Maybe I have made a mistake" or "Maybe I should wait." We know the devil is there to encourage thoughts like that. Once the sale is made, you have had prayer in the home, enrolled the family in the Bible course, and gotten referrals of others who would appreciate this service, reassure them as you leave that they have made the right decision and that the Lord is going to bless them with this material in their home.

You may occasionally lose a sale because of buyer's remorse.

80 SERVING GOD'S PURPOSE IN OUR GENERATION

However, some of these lost sales can be saved by going back and seeing the family again. If you can not resell them on the same unit, try selling part of the unit. Often these sales are lost because we do not properly reassure the prospects while in the home. Above all be sure to thank them for their business. It is amazing how many do not do this.

Often I tell a little child before I leave, "You know you are very fortunate to have parents who will get these books for you. I call in homes where parents don't feel that these beautiful books are important. You should hug your mother and thank her for getting these." More than once, I've seen a child go over, at my suggestion, hug the parents and thank them for getting the books. I have looked at the parent's eyes, and they become misty. When this happens, you can be sure it's not very likely that family is going to let some negative influence of the devil convince them later that they made a mistake.

Another statement I use sometimes in reassuring the people is, "Mrs. Jones, God in time will honor us not for how much money we put in our children's pockets, but how much character we put in their lives."

I like to also reassure people in my prayer that they have made the right decision. As we pray before we leave the home, our prayer should not be too long, but long enough to thank God for the opportunity of meeting these people and to reassure them through the prayer that this is God's will for their home. So we assure them twice, once during the prayer and again before we walk out. Reassure with a thank you note. Mail the note the day you make the sale. That note will arrive before the books are mailed. This reassures the person again that you are sincere and they made the right decision.

9. Use Reserve Points

One lady literature evangelist said after she closed a sale, "You know, that lady only said, "No" five times to me before she purchased." Having reserve points is knowing more about your books than just your presentation. Use closing stories and don't give up too soon.

Sometimes when people say No, what they really mean is, "I need to be convinced still more." Never take the first no. Look at it in a positive way and just turn it around. Instead of no, turn it into on and go on and close again. Now if people want to buy before you get to the end of your presentation, don't be like the literature evangelist who said, "But wait, you haven't heard all of my presentation yet!" There are some people who are impatient, and we must close earlier in our presentation. Experience will help you learn how to handle these people.

While taking a Big Week in West Palm Beach, Florida, I had a difficult time contacting a certain lady. Just before my week was over, I found her home. She said she could not see me that day, but to come back early the next morning because she was interested. Since she said be at her house at seven the next morning, I was there at seven. There are two lessons I want to share with you from this story.

Lesson one is if somebody wants to see you at a hour that is inconvenient to you, be there, for that's the Lord's appointment. An insurance salesman told of a contrary farmer who said that the only time that he would talk with him would be just before he milked the cows at 4:30 A. M. in the morning. The insurance salesman was there at 4:00 a.m. and sold insurance to that dairy farmer. I was working with a literature evangelist, when a mother said, "I'm interested but I can't talk with you today. You must come back to see me at 8:00 A. M. in the morning." The literature evangelist told me why he was so hesitant about coming back. He said, "That's the time I normally exercise." Now, I believe that we should have a definite time for everything but if someone wants to see your product, which could save them and their family for eternity, you be there at a time that is convenient for them! You can pick up your routine of exercise and study the next morning. Divine appointment cannot wait.

Lesson two from this story is: Don't quit closing when you still have an interest. I gave the lady in West Palm Beach my $2,000 presentation and asked for an order of $600. She showed a lot of interest, but couldn't make a decision. I closed on her, and each time she would slap her hand on the oil cloth that covered her table and say "I just don't know." I asked the Lord for more words to help me, to recall some story that would show her the benefits of these books for her and her grandchildren. I tried to close again and again. Each time she would slap the oil cloth on the table and say, "I just don't know. Maybe I should think it over. I want these, but I think I'd better think it over." I felt impressed that if she did not make the decision now, she would never get the books. I stayed with her, sent another prayer to heaven and closed again. Again she made the same statement and slapped the oil cloth that was covering the table. Eventually she said, after many, many closes, "Okay, I'm going to get these books. How much is it again?" Then she pulled the oil cloth off the table. Under it were 20 dollar bills layers deep. I don't know how much money she had under that oil cloth but it was hundreds of dollars, possibly thousands.

Each time I would try closing the sale, she was slapping her money, thinking about the cash hidden right under that oil cloth. She was weighing the benefits of these books throughout eternity against the loss of the money that lay just under her hand. Fortunately, the Lord impressed her that the books were much more valuable than cold hard cash. Don't give up too soon. Remember, if at first you don't close but still have an interest, close and close again and pray for the power of the Holy Spirit.

10. Seldom Make A Call Back

Seldom make a call back when you have made a full presentation. In economics there is something called the point of diminishing returns. In our work it also true when closing a sale. The best time to close a sale is the first time you make a presentation. Each time you come back and talk to the prospect the chances of your closing the sale diminishes. Also, the greater the lapse of time between the calls, the more the opportunity diminishes. Surveys by some workers show that only 5 to 10 percent ever buy on call backs. You may occasionally get a call back sale and it may encourage you to make more call backs. In doing this, you waste time that could be used seeing someone who is really interested. Personally, I almost never come back unless the prospect makes a partial deposit or I was unable to see the spouse.

"When persons who are under conviction are not brought to a decision at the earliest period possible, there is danger that the conviction will gradually wear away..." Evan. p. 298.

The man we looked at earlier has become your friend. He likes and trusts you. He sees his need and understands the eternal benefits your product will give him and his family. You started right so your close was easy. He not only is your friend, but now may your neighbor throughout out eternity.

Chapter 8

"Behold upon the mountains the feet of him that bringeth good tidings, that publisheth peace!"
Nahum 1:15, KJV.

Answering Objections

Many literature evangelists dread objections. But often an objection is a signal showing that the prospect wants you to explain more and reassure him again that he is making the right decision. What he may be saying is, "I really want to buy these and you seem honorable. Help me decide what I know I should decide."

I was canvassing with Velma Welty in Cheyenne, Wyoming. We had closed a sale after many objections. As we left the home, she said to me, "Do you realize you never answered her objections?" I didn't realize what I had done. The lady was not actually objecting. She was just wanting to know more. Usually when a prospect does not buy, the objection that is given is not the real reason that the sale wasn't made. The late Judge Ziglar, an international sales trainer, once said, "The reason most people do not buy is that they do not fully understand the proposition." Possibly, you've not made the method of payment clear or they may honestly have some objection you need to explain. Maybe you need to emphasize the benefits one more time.

Remember, people do not buy facts or features no matter how accurate they are. People buy the benefits that those facts will bring them. You must be able to paint the benefits so that they can see them in their mind's eye. The following are some examples of the difference between a fact and a benefit. After you a state fact ask yourself the question, "So what?" If you have not shown how those facts are benefits, then you have not answered the "so what."

People buy benefits not facts.

1. **Fact**—*The Bible Story* books cover the entire Bible.

Benefit—These beautiful volumes cover the entire Bible narrative which means they just make the Bible come alive and make it so much more understandable for your child. One mother said to us, "I never knew so much about the Bible until I got these for the children."

2. **Fact**—These covers are washable.

Benefit—These covers are durable and meant to last a life time. In fact, you can take a damp cloth and wash them off. Someone has called these peanut butter and jelly proof. Maybe your children won't touch them with dirty hands. (Smile as you say this.) If you take care of these volumes, even your grandchildren will be able to use them.

3. **Fact**—*Bible Readings* has 4,000 questions and answers.

Benefit—*Bible Reading* has over 4,000 Bible questions and answers which means almost any topic that you want to study can be found here in an organized way. This saves hours of using a concordance looking up each text. Many Sunday School teachers and ministers have said that they find this to be a real blessing in their Bible study and class preparation.

Give an example of someone you know or a story that has been shared with you. When you state a fact, you may bridge that fact to the benefit with the words "which means" or "so that" or "therefore." If you will tack these words on at the end of every fact that you state, it will help you to always state the benefit of the fact.

Nail down some of the benefits in the prospect's mind by getting an agreement after stating the benefit. An example would be after showing one of your favorite pictures to say, "Isn't this a beautiful painting? The old saying that one picture is worth a

1000 words is really true especially for children isn't it?" Or after showing *Bible Readings For The Home* say, "Mr. Jones, this would be a real help in your Bible study class you were mentioning earlier, wouldn't it?" You should not nail down every benefit, but some of them. Remember, every nod of agreement or little yes makes the big yes at the close that much easier.

Now in answering objections, state the benefit and if possible, as mentioned in closing the sale, try to use a third person story. Your prospect can always see himself in another person's experience without you pointing directly at him and making him uncomfortable.

Retired publishing leader, Elder Russell Thomas, shared this story with me. Many years ago when he was learning to fly, he was coming in for his solo landing. His nervous trainer shouted at the top of his voice, "Don't crash man. Make another circle!" He pulled the plane up, made another circle and then landed smoothly. When closing a sale, if we see that we are going to crash after asking our closing question, make another circle. Go around again. Maybe even lay your books aside and talk with the prospect about some of her interests. I have done this many times. I have had prospects tell me that they were simply not interested. I laid my books aside and even put my contract pad back in my briefcase and sat visiting a while. (By the way, when showing them your contract, don't say "contract," say "agreement.") Literature Evangelist David Sigamani, after a very spiritual canvas, hands the prospect the contract and says "this is your commitment, okay it here please." Don't say "sign," say "okay the agreement," or "okay the paper work." Words such as *contract* and *sign* make some people nervous. Do not refer to "customers you sold" but "people you have served." Rather than "your books will be delivered in two weeks," say "you will receive these beautiful volumes in two weeks." This sets people at ease. You may be dealing with an individual who does not like making decisions quickly. I would talk about the interest of the prospect and when the opportunity comes, I will say something like, "Mr. Jones, I was thinking about our earlier conversation and how you said how you could see how these volumes could really be of benefit to you. You know one man that I visited told me "_____" (Then I use one of my third party stories). Rather than crashing, I make another circle. I will ask a closing question again and hopefully have answered his objection.

> **When closing do not crash, make another circle, show another benefit, close again.**

In order to make the landing as smooth as possible, we must find out, if possible, what the prospect's real objection is. This may not come out immediately. There are several simple methods that you can memorize. You could, of course, just ignore the objection and continue showing benefits. But, the better way is to try to find out what it really is. When smoking out the objection, and answering it directly, you should do the following:

1. Treat the person's objection with respect, no matter how ridiculous it seems to you.

2. Look directly at the person when answering the objections. Listen carefully to what he has to say and read facial expressions. Sometimes the expressions will say something different than what the mouth is saying.

3. Remain spiritual, calm and pleasant.

4. Above all, do not argue. Never forget this truth, "Win an argument, lose a friend." Sales are made on agreements, not on disagreements.

5. Keep your third party story or answer brief, but applicable to the objection.

6. Bring the conversation back to a closing question like, "If you were to get these, would you take care of the entire investment today or just the minimum deposit?" Or try this, "Would you like the complete set or our basic unit?" If you are new and inexperienced, it may be easier just to use the same closing question again. People won't mind and probably won't remember that you've asked it earlier.

I've found that the objections you receive in America, Africa, or Europe, are about the same. The objections that people raise are seldom unique. Occasionally you may find something unique, but generally they are about the same.

In answering objections, "We wrestle not against flesh and blood, but against principalities, against powers, against the rulers of the darkness of this world. Whenever a book is presented that will expose error, Satan is close by the side of the one to whom it is offered and urges reasons why it should not be accepted." CM p. 115. In answering objections, we must always be in the attitude of prayer. "But a divine agency is at work to influence minds in favor of the light. Ministering angels will oppose their power to that of Satan." CM p. 115. Following are some methods that I find particularly useful. I have learned some of these from experience and some are borrowed from fellow workers. I don't remember where I first heard many of them. Others are from reading books such as Zig Ziglar, Dale Carnegie, Peter Lowe, Tom Hopkins and one of my mentors Paul Jensen.

You will notice that the key to answering objections is direct or implied questions. Go through the four Gospels and observe how many times Jesus answered questions this way. He was our example in this also. Some suggestions in secular sales books may not apply to you, but as my father would have said, "Chew up the meat and spit out the bones." Some of us who have worked many years forget what we used to do and it is always good to go back and re-learn methods that work. As King Solomon said, "There is nothing new under the sun." Ecclesiastes 1:9. Former U.S. President Harry Truman once said, "The only thing that is new is the history that we have forgotten." Most of the following methods are as old as Aristotle and Socrates. Try them, they still work. Human nature is the same everywhere.

Smoking Out the Real Objection

1. *Repeat the question approach.*

Looking directly at the customer, lower your voice and repeat exactly what the customer has said. Again wait quietly for the prospect's answer. This puts the answering of the objection back on the customer. "The price is too high?" There was not a question mark after the remark when the customer said it. But by your repeating it back, you put a question mark on your face and in the way that you express it. In answering in this manner, many times the customer will go on to answer his own objection or share with you some other problem that he has which may have nothing to do with the price.

Through the years, it has been my experience that at this point in closing sales that many prospects, intentional or not, will lie to you. So do not accept most objections at face value unless you hear them three times.

2. *"Is there anything else?" answer to objections.*

"Mr. Prospect, other than price is there anything else that would keep you from investing in these tonight?" (Again, be quiet, look at the person and let him answer your question.) Now if Mr. Prospect says there is nothing else and you go on to answer the price objection and show him how he could have these, and then he comes up with another objection, it is time to move, because he is not being honest with you. If, however, price is his real reason, then you can do your best to answer it.

Go on to break the objection down. "Mr. Prospect, is it the total amount that you would invest in these volumes or just the initial deposit today?" (Wait for the answer.) Always reassure the prospect of the blessings to him and his family and let him know you will do all that you can to work with him on it. It may be that you will have to sell a smaller set or even a single volume. But continue trying to make the decision based on agreements.

3. *"Feel, felt, found" answer to any objection.*

This one is easy to learn. If we remember these three words: *feel, felt, found,* we can use them any time in answering objections. If you feel a little under pressure because of something the prospect has said and can't think of an answer, just think, *feel, felt,* and *found.* Remembering them will help you to answer many objections.

Objection "I want to think it over." (This is the most universal and hated objection that people will hear in any line of sales work. It is vague and almost never the truth.)

1. **Feel**—"I understand how you **feel.**"
2. **Felt**—"Others **felt** as you when I first presented these."
3. **Found**—"But this is what they **found.**"

Tell a story of how someone who purchased from you previously used these volumes. Possibly a story that your leader or fellow literature evangelists has shared with you or anything you may find useful from this book. Again, I urge using the powerful third person stories in which the prospect can see himself, and give him a choice again for time of delivery, cash or initial investment. Close again.

4. *Is "I want to think it over," the real objection?*

"I understand how you feel. May I ask you a question? (Pause.) Other than price, is there anything that will keep you from making a decision today?" Listen and you may smoke out the real objection.

5. *"If you were to get this" answer to objection.*

"I understand how you feel. May I ask you a question? If you were to get these today, what would be the main reason for doing so?" (Listen carefully and build on what you are told. Continue using third-party stories. Close and ask for a decision again.

6. *Answer to objection, "Could you come back later?"*

"I understand how you feel. Let me ask you a question. On a scale of 1-10, where are you when it comes to investing in these today?" (Pause and listen.) "I'm about a three." "Mr. Prospect, what will it take to move you up the scale to a seven or eight?" Smile, listen carefully. They may give you the answer to what is really holding them back. Sell a benefit and close with a choice again.

7. *Answer to objection, "These are too expensive."*

"Mr. Prospect, compared to what?" Again, we want to find out what the prospect is thinking. Remember heaven is weighing in the balance.

8. *Answer to objection, "I want to talk with my priest/ minister first."*

Lower your voice and ask, "What specifically do you have a question about?"

9. *Answer to objection, "I shouldn't get these now. I must wait or I can't decide right now."*

"Mr. Prospect, what would happen if you did?" or "What would prevent you from doing it now?" One literature evangelist said he asked this question and the lady answered, "We are going to buy a house, and we are saving for it." The LE looked at her, smiled and said, "Linda do you really believe the Lord would keep you from having that house if you got these for your family?" She saw how foolish her objection was and replied, "You are right. I will take them."

10. *Answer to objection, "We always pray about every decision we make."*

(This is one that the fundamentalists love to give.) You could answer with method number one by lowering your voice and saying, "Always?" A similar objection to this is, "We never buy anything unless we can pay for it all at once." Again just lower your voice, look at them and say, "Never?" Another similar objection is, "Every time we make a decision like this, we always sleep on it for a few days." Again, look at the prospect and repeat, "Every time?"

Les McCoy Assistant Publishing Leader in the Florida Conference, first shared this method with me. When people use words like *never*, *always*, *every*, just repeat the word "never," "always," "every." This works even with your children. Your child may say, "How come I always have to do the dishes?" You say, "Always, son?"

Les came in late and very tired one night. As he undressed, he just dropped his clothes on the floor and crawled into bed. His wife said, Les, you always just drop your clothes in the floor." Les had just learned this technique. He said, "Always, Honey?" She replied, "Well, not always." Les then explained what he had just done. He may have had to sleep on the couch that night!

11. When you cannot think of an answer to the objection—1.

Sometimes when a prospect gives an objection and you cannot think of an answer, you can simply look at him and ask the question, "Why?"

12. When you cannot think of an answer to the objection—2.

Some objections given may simply be answered by, "Does it really matter?" Use this if you don't believe it is a real objection. Many times the prospect will say, "Oh no, not really."

13. Turn the objection into a reason for buying.

Example 1— "My children are too young." — "Mr. Prospect, that is the very reason many of our satisfied customers purchase these. They find that what educators and child psychologists have said for years is true. The early years are the most important in teaching character. Psychologist tell us the most important thing we can do for our children other than hugging them is to read to them. No TV or video can replace the human voice or touch. When you read to your child you teach your ideals and morals and these thoughts are instilled more permanently than any other way."

Example 2— "We don't have children yet." "Mr. Prospect, this is the very reason many of our satisfied customers purchase these.

They found that it was easier to invest in these before their children arrived. In fact, so many parents have told us through the years 'I never knew so much about the Bible until I got these for the children.' "

Example 3— "I'd like to know what Father O'Hare would say."

"Mr. Prospect, that's the very reason many of our satisfied customers purchase these books. Catholic schools throughout the country have used them through the years and found them one of the best tools for teaching the Bible." Almost any objection can be turned into a reason for buying.

14. Shock answer to objection

This is one that will work only on special occasions, but is another one Les McCoy has shared with me, and it worked for him. I'll call this the shock answer. Les was giving a presentation and the mother loved the books, but the father was agitated that his wife was interested in buying these books for the children. Finally, when Les came to the close and quoted the price of $500, the man stood up and said "What! These books cost $500?" in a loud voice. Les stood up raised his hand and said in just as an excited voice. "I know it, sir, I can't believe it either. I don't know how they produce these so cheap." The man looked shocked, sat down and his wife ordered the books without any more opposition from her husband.

15. Divide the cost by the time used method.

Prospect: "I know these books are good but I don't know that I will get $700 value from them." Answer: "I understand how you feel. Many of my customers felt this way when they first looked at the books. But then they began thinking of how much the value of these beautiful stories would be over ten years. You see if you just read one story nightly and two on Sunday, it will take you a year to go through the set. That's only about a dollar per story. But many families have told us that they've read these over and over through the years and if you were to use these ten years, that would only cost you ten cents per day. If you think of the character that this would instill in your children, and how they would help meet the temptations that come their way, ten cents a day would be a small investment, wouldn't it?" Another effective story for this objection that I have used for years came from a lady in St. Louis, Missouri. The lady had *The Bible Story* books and told me that she worked and was raising her son alone. She said when she came home from work at night she was just too tired to read to him. Her little boy would beg her to read these books to him. One evening she told him several times, "Son I'm just too tired and have so much to do. I can't do it tonight." He turned to her and said, "You know mamma, a story a day keeps the devil away." She read him a story! "Mr. Prospect, that's really true, isn't it? A story a day DOES keep the devil away and it does really help to instill those wholesome character traits in our children. They need to meet the temptations that young people have to face today. Do you think it will be worth ten cents a day to have these in your home?"

16. *Compare spiritual food to physical food.*

Compare spiritual value to physical value of the cost of food in your area. Prospect: "I can't afford it." "I understand how you feel, Mr. Prospect. Many of my customers felt that way at first. But may I ask you a question? Do you spend $40 or $50 on food for a week?" Many prospects will answer, "Yes, I spend one hundred dollars a week on food." "Well, Mr. Prospect, if we only feed our children once a week, they would starve to death, wouldn't they?" (Prospect will agree.) If they go to church every week, it is still only one day. With these volumes, you can feed your family daily. And if you were to use them for five years, it would only be a cost of twenty cents a day. You can afford that, can't you Mr. or Mrs. Prospect?"

17. *Answer the objection with a letter from a happy customer.*

The following three letters are great examples of this. I challenge you to try these or you may acquire better ones through your own experience. But remember a written testimony is one of the most powerful arguments. Again it is easy to start your answer to the objection with Feel, Felt, Found. Be sure to read these letters with feeling and look them in the eye when you ask the closing question.

Letter 1:

This could be used for the objections: "I can't find time to read to my children." "I don't know if my children would use them." "I am an adult and I don't know if these would help me," or " I am a grandparent and it is my children's job to train their children." I will answer the latter.

"Mrs. Jones, I understand how you feel. Some of the grandparents I have called on felt that way at first, but listen to what this satisfied grandmother said in a letter sent recently."

"In 1956 my first little girl was born; in '58 another little girl. I realized I had to set an example for my children, so we started reading them the Bible, telling it in our own words, that they could understand. I ran across your *Bible Story* books at my doctor's office and ordered a set. Well, during that time I had three more girls making a total of five in all. I also purchased the *Bedtime Stories*. Until my children married and left home, we had our nightly devotion. It always had to be from these books. I can't tell you how many times we read the entire set through. But it was many, many times. Now that they have children, they're all wanting the one set of books. So, you understand why I've had to order four more sets of all of the books. They all wanted the old set. I started with the oldest believing that they would mean more to her. So she gets the old set to the dismay of the others. They are almost completely worn out but still readable. Now I need four sets of the *Uncle Arthur's Bedtime Stories*. Add it to my account please. At least they can't say, I didn't try. As an adult I enjoyed the books. When you send these, I'll have a little more room on my book shelf. I praise God for the company that put these books out. May many more children be blessed as mine were. Now my grandchildren can't fuss over a certain book when they come—I won't have them here. They'll have them at home. Oh boy . . .."

Yours in Christ, Lenora C. Baker

"Mrs. Jones, both children and grandchildren are an inheritance from the Lord. In this day and age children need all the wholesome and character building material they can get to meet life's temptations. Wouldn't you agree? If you were to get these today would you want one set or one for each of your children's family?"

Letter 2:

Use this letter when the prospect says, "I never buy anything on time. If I don't have the money at the time I don't get it!" "Mr. Jones, I understand how you feel. Many of the people I have called on felt that way at first but then considered this different than just some ordinary purchase. They looked at this in the light of eternity and what it would do for them and their family not only here but hereafter. It never pays to put off spiritual decisions. I want to share with you a recent letter from Mrs. Hamrick to one of our representatives."

Dear Greg:

"Thank you for responding to my request to see the *Bible Story* books and helping me make my purchase. They are books I have wanted for 30 years.

My first opportunity to have these books came years and years ago when a middle-aged gentleman came to my home. He made his presentation to my husband, our three small children and me. Our fourth child was in diapers at the time. We wanted to buy the books, but my husband told the salesman he did not have the cash that day. That very day my husband had bought a new motorcycle and was broke! He would have purchased the books if he had the cash. He refused to buy anything on credit. He had paid cash for his motorcycle!

My husband said he could buy the books the following Tuesday— exactly one week later. I was terribly disappointed because the books were beautiful, and we were raising a Christian family. The salesman also looked disappointed. My husband assured him, "I'll buy them next Tuesday." The salesman replied, "Mr. Hamrick, you may not be here next Tuesday."

The following Tuesday at 6:10 p.m., approximately the same time the salesman had been at our house, a week earlier, my husband was killed on his motorcycle. I never got to buy the books for my children. Now 30 years later, I can have them for my 11 grandchildren!"

The books are beautiful, and I thank you sincerely.
Cynthia Hamrick

Again ask your closing question.

Letter 3:

Use this letter when some says, "I am not sure if I will get my money's worth," or "I am not sure if we will take time to read these." This is a great letter and short, and if the people have a heart in their chest that the Lord can touch, this letter will do it.

"Mrs. Jones, I understand how you feel, no doubt Mrs. Adkins felt that way when she first thought about getting these books for her home. Her grammar and spelling are not too good, but her priorities are right. She sent us this letter recently.

> "Home Health Education Service: "35 years ago I bought a set of your books. At that time we raised 10 children. Ever night we would all gather around the table. Ever night I would read a Bible story and then then we would get down on our knees and have prayer. I raised my family on them books. I red (read) them thur 6 times. In the later years, they all grown up and they all gone now, I gave those 10 books to 2 of my grandaugthers about three years ago. Oh how I missed them dear books. But thanks to Mr. Johnson another set. Praise the Lord. I am 70 years old."
> Yours Truly, Mrs. Basil R. Adkins

Mrs. Jones, do think her children will be better employees, better husbands and wives and people in their communities because of the influence of reading books? This Mother was giving her children a moral compass. With all the temptations that our young people have today, they need all the help they can get, don't they?" Again give them a choice and ask for the order.

18. Objections After The Sale

Occasionally a customer may be upset and want to cancel an order after the sale. This may be because of buyer's remorse, prejudice or simply a misunderstanding. If you have to go back to see a customer, never go back in an argumentive manner. Remain spiritual and listen carefully to what he has to say. Once you hear him out apologize for any misunderstanding, show him again the benefits these will be to his family. An apology disarms many argumentive people. People expect you to be on the defensive, and when you are not they have to defend their point, if they have one.

I was working with a literature evangelist, and we sold a very sincere lady a large order. She assured us we did not need to see her husband as this would be her decision. Unfortunately, her husband was not of the same opinion. The next day he called me, upset that his wife bought the books. I listened to him and then apologized, assuring him that our intention was only to leave books that would build strong Christian families. She loved the books so much and thought he would also. I apologized again. I could hear his resentment lowering as we continued our phone conversation. He told me I did not need to apologize. I apologized again and shared more benefits with him. Each sincere apology, followed by a testimony of the benefit of the books was melting his case. Finally he said, "Mr Beckworth I am sorry I bothered you. We will keep the books. You had no way of knowing about my idiosyncrasies."

Nothing you learn will work all of the time. But if you learn several of these methods, some of them will work some of the time.

The following quote is from Zig Ziglar's book, *On Selling* p. 233 "Research from Dr. Herb True of Notre Dame reveals that forty-six percent of the salespeople he interviewed ask for the order once and then quit; twenty-four percent ask for the order twice before giving up; fourteen percent ask the third time; and twelve percent 'hang in there' to make four attempts before throwing in the proverbial towel. That's a total of ninety-six percent who quit after four closing attempts, and yet the same research shows that a full sixty percent of all sales are made after the fifth closing attempt. Since the percentage of salespeople not asking for the sale the necessary five times equals ninety six percent, it's obvious that four percent are making sixty percent of the sales (and sixty percent of the commissions)."

There are many good books you can buy and read that will help you sell. A book that is a real benefit to you should be read once a year. I like Zig Ziglar's books. He may help in selling from A to Z (no pun intended) but it is still the Alpha and Omega that keeps my vision clear and is the greatest help in answering objection. Call upon Him in prayer. It is the fastest thing in the world, and the surest help.

Chapter 9

"Because I will publish the name of the Lord:
ascribe ye greatness unto my God."
Deut. 32:3

Remembering Names

Remembering names is a real asset in Christian salesman-ship and leadership. Everyone's name is important; at least it's important to the person who has that name. Remember what I stated earlier: everyone is wearing an invisible tag stat-ing "Make me feel important." Nothing makes people feel more important than being called by their name.

This is an area where I personally struggle. I seem to be able to remember many facts, experiences, and other material, but not people's names. But can this be improved?

I have been impressed with many of our church leaders abil-ity to remember so many people's names. Elder Neal C. Wilson has this ability. I have read stories of Elder Spicer when he was General Conference president. While visiting mission fields, he would look at pictures and memorize the names of the missionar-ies and even their children. When he visited the compounds, he could call each one by name making them feel important and encouraging them to stay by the work.

The most incredible person that I have ever known for remem-bering names was Elder R. H. Pierson, General Conference presi-dent. When I was in Africa, he returned after being gone for 20 years. We had rented a large church and there was a huge turnout. Everyone loved and respected him and wanted to shake his hand. Many came away absolutely amazed that he could remember their names after 20 years. A fellow worker told me that he had not seen Elder Pierson for 20 years and when he went through the greeting line, Elder Pierson called him by his full name and told that it was good to see him. I have to believe that was a special gift that God gave Elder Pierson, but I am also sure that he cultivated it. All the books that I have read state that remembering names is a skill that can be learned. Be sure those people whose service was remembered feel better about themselves and church leadership because their leader remembered their name.

There are some unique individuals in history such as Napoleon. It is said that he could remember thousands of soldiers by name. Charles Schwab claimed to have known all eight thousand of his employees at the mill by name. Charles W. Elliott, who was president of Harvard University for 40 years, had a reputation of knowing all the students by name each year. These individuals are phenomenal exceptions, but all of us can improve this skill.

Ellen White has said some things about those of us who are forgetful that are not too complimentary. To improve this, she has suggested, "Let the more important passages of Scripture be committed to memory...Though if at first the memory be defective, it will gain strength by exercise." CD, p. 512. "All minds are not naturally constituted alike. We are varied minds; some are strong upon certain points and weak on others. These deficiencies, so apparent, need not, should not exist. If those who possess them would strengthen the weak point of their character by cultivating and exercise, they would become strong." 3T, p. 33. In the school of the prophets, she said, "The use of figures and symbols caused the lessons given to be more firmly fixed in the memory." PP, p. 592. Some writers suggest the secret of remembering names lies in the very brief period of time that we stand face to face with another person. At that time, that is the most important person to you. First of all, God has brought the two of you together and has allowed your paths to cross. If that meeting is important, so is that person's name. One author has said that when you meet that person, blot everything else out, then zero in on that name. Ignore all other distractions.

Recently, I met a sales representative for Worthington Food. I met him in an Adventist Book Center and had a brief encounter.

He repeated my name five times in our conversation. I left knowing what he was trying to do. He was trying to remember my name. I also left knowing that I should have been doing the same thing. At this moment, I cannot recall his name. But if I had said it five times, I probably could.

Here are some suggestions for remembering names:

1. Hear the name and pronounce it correctly.

Allow that name to make an impression on your mind. Repeat it and possibly spell it if you have a question. Do not be afraid to ask the person, "How do you spell that?"

2. Associate that name with something.

Whatever you can visualize beside that name or draw a picture in your mind of the name, no matter how far out or bizarre, do that. Some suggest the wilder the picture you draw of the person, the better. That will help you in remembering the name. I once heard of a fellow who tried remembering someone's name by association. He met a Mr. Claypoole. He began thinking—clay, dirt, mud, pool, water, mud-hole. Unfortunately, when he went to introduce the man, he got his bizarre association confused with the name and introduced him as Mr. Mudhole! Make sure that you recall the name, not just the associations that you attach to the name!

3. Repetition

As you talk together, as the sales rep did with me, try repeating the individual's name several times. Perhaps you could introduce the individual to someone else. This will give you the opportunity to pronounce the name. Be sure that you do it distinctly.

Names are important to Christ: (Revelation 20:15, Revelation 21:27.) "He knows us by name." D.A., p. 479. "God knows you by name" M.L., p. 291. When you hear a name, instantly you have a mental picture of someone and their characteristics. The same is true of our Lord, "Each believer's name is graven on the palms of his hands." F.E. p.273. According to Revelation 2:17, we will also receive new names and we will carry these throughout eternity. If God emphasizes my name, why should I not do my best to remember the name of those I hope to win for His kingdom?

Chapter 10

*"...He...began to publish in Decapolis
how great things Jesus had done for him:
and all men did marvel." Mark 5:20, KJV.*

Your Goals and God's Providence

G od gives opportunities; success depends upon the use made of them." PK p. 486. Law and grace, mercy and justice, while different, work together and both are needed. One would not be useful without the other. Some people see goal setting as contrary to God's will and not allowing for His providence. But the truth is that goals and providence work together. We must have some standard we set to reach, at the same time, allowing space for God's providence.

Joshua understood this combination. "Joshua had received the promise that God would surely overthrow these enemies of Israel, yet he put forth an earnest effort as though success depended upon the armies of Israel alone. He did all that human energy could do, and then he cried in faith for divine aid. The secret of success is the union of divine power with human effort." CM, p. 106.

I once was listening to a group of literature evangelists talk, and heard one say, "I drove for two hours before the Lord impressed me to stop at this house and knock." I wanted to jump up and shout, "Friend, was it the Lord who caused you to waste those two hours?" Goals helps us use our time more efficiently.

Some workers have told me they cannot get more calls in because of circumstances. Circumstances gets more blame for failure than the Devil. I read in a publishing newsletter two great questions for all of us. First, "Is there anything you could do to make your circumstances worse?" The obvious answer is, "Yes." Second, "Then is there any thing you could do to make your circumstances better?" To this we must all say, "yes" also. Apply these questions to your work or your home. Listen to Ellen White's counsel on circumstances. "Man can shape his circumstances, but circumstances should not shape the man. We should seize upon the circumstances as instruments with which to work. We are master to them, but should not permit them to master us." 3T, p. 497.

It would appear she believed in goals. Replace "rules' with "goals" in this next statement. "Persons who have not acquired habits of industry and economy of time, should have set rules to prompt them." GW, p. 292.

> **"Man can shape his circumstances, but circumstances should not be allowed to shape the man."—*Gospel Workers,* p. 292.**

Goals help us to be organized and save time. If you are going to be goal oriented you need to be a list maker. Every literature evangelist should have a note pad and pen nearby whether at work or lying in bed reading. When you think of something you need to do, write it down. When a bright idea strikes you, jot it down. I always get more done on the days I make a good list. People who make lists always get more done because they are more organized. Now being organized comes more naturally to some than others. But all of us can improve. Have you gone on a vacation or long trip that you had to put a lot of planning into? What did you do the preceding days or even weeks? Did you write a list of things to do? Did you get more done in those days than normal? Did you spend less time watching television? Did you feel good about what you accomplished in that span of time? Weren't you more enthusiastic than normal? What if you a made list like that every day and used your time as wisely? Wouldn't life have more zing and joy?

I read about a top executive in a large company who had an almost photographic memory. He said, "I do not forget many things, but I still make a list because it helps me be organized." Make a list and look at it regularly. Every literature evangelist should have a note pad at all times as we never know when we will find an interest and need to write their name and address down.

The following is a story illustrating the waste of genius when goals are absent. In 1516, James Quinton was born in Scotland, and as he grew up, he became known as the world's greatest intellect. At the age of 13, he had a Bachelor's Degree and at 17, a Master's Degree. People considered him a human encyclopedia. It is reported that by the age of 20, he could tell people literally everything about anything that was known at that time. He had a photographic memory. Those who knew him and were close to him said that he never forgot anything. He was a speed reader before the term was invented. It is said that he could read a 500 page book in two hours and write an accurate account of its contents. When he was 23, he was hired to tutor a prince. And at the age of 24, he was killed in a drunken brawl. Those who documented his life said, "We've lost a giant intellect; a man of many talents." But what if he had lived to be 100, what would he have accomplished? Probably nothing because he had no goals in his life. When asked once what he wanted to accomplish, he stated, "It doesn't matter. Whatever happens, happens."

If you do not have a goal, you are sure to reach it! Write your goals down and look at them often enough to keep them fixed in your mind. This helps save time and avoid distractions. Make goals for family, finance, reading, health, and above all your work. When goals are well defined and written down you can measure your accomplishments. Goals should be realistic but stretch you beyond your present accomplishments. They should be set with much thought and prayer.

Goals motivate us. Through the years I've watched many people in the literature work. Invariably, people of ordinary talent who discipline their time and have definite aims always accomplish more than the most talented and brilliant without discipline and goals. Goals fixed in our thoughts help us stay motivated. Motivation produces discipline. Discipline produces habits. Habits produce goals accomplished. "More than any natural endowment, the habits . . . decide whether a man will be victorious or vanquished in the battle of life." DA, p. 101.

> *"Habits...decide...the battle of life."—Desire of Ages,* p. 101.

Motivation, though, is not a permanent fixture in our character. We lose it at times, but if our goals are written and reviewed, we are more likely to maintain impetus. Motivation is like eating, we need to partake each day. Put your goals on 3 by 5 cards. These are easy to carry and glance at.

Writing this manuscript has been a series of losing my motivation and picking it up again. I tried to do a certain amount each day and week but after weeks of rewriting and rewriting, I would lay it aside for periods of time. During a hectic time last summer I set it down for three months. I always kept it where I could see it and would be reminded of the long term goal.

I wish I had stuck to my schedule. Fortunately, I got back on track and finished the manuscript. Once we make an exception and break an important routine, it becomes easier to make the exception again and soon the exception becomes the rule. A good example of this is people who cannot make it to church on time or those who say they still believe but they just got out of the habit of going. Life is richer in every way when you are committed to wholesome habits.

If you want to change a habit in your routine do it for 18 working days and it will become a habit. Repetition becomes automation or habit.

Zig Ziglar tells how he kept his goal of losing weight on his mind every day. He discovered they never use rotund guys to advertise men's underwear. All the models were slim and the size he wanted to be. He cut out one of the advertisements and cut the model's head off and put his own picture on it. He then taped that picture on his bathroom mirror. Every day when he shaved he was reminded of how he would look if he stuck to his daily goal of exercise and diet.

Goals help us be persistent. Former U. S. President Calvin Coolidge said, "Nothing in the world can take the place of persistence. Talent will not; nothing is more common than unsuccessful men of talent. Genius will not: unrewarded genius is almost a proverb. Education will not; the world is full of educated derelicts. Persistence and determination alone are omnipotent."

Do you think persistence is something you are born with? Is it just in some people's genes and not in others? To hear some folks make excuses you would believe it. A worker said to me, "I wish I were as disciplined as our leading literature evangelist." My response was, "You can be. It is learned." Persistence, discipline, faithfulness, enthusiasm, consistency, diligence and hard work are not inherited. These are a gift from God only if we take action. These are learned skills! We learn them as we take action each hour and day. These gifts follow our action. Under "Enthusiasm" in Chapter 6 the formula to acquire these traits is given. "Act as if" and you will be.

> **Persistence, patience, faithfulness, discipline, good manners, enthusiasm, diligence, and hard work are learned skills.**

We must have a big picture that we are shooting at, but it is the taking care of the little things that make the big things fall in place. We have all heard the saying "Take care of the little things, and the big things will take care of themselves." Before I was converted, I played organized football for seven years. Every coach I played for would emphasize the little things. Everyone of them would say, "If we block, if we tackle, if we hand the ball off; if we do all of these little things right, the big game will fall into place." They drilled fundamentals over and over. All of the team loved to play football but hated the monotony of drills. But the drills are what produced good players. Everything revolves around fundamentals. If you don't believe it, just ask any engineer who has designed an engine or an architect who has designed a great building. In our Christian selling, we must have a time to start and a time to quit. We need time for family and for study, exercise and rest. Life must be balanced, but often the area that will be sacrificed by most people when there is not someone else telling them what to do, is the area of work habits.

The parable of the talents in Luke chapter 19 emphasizes how important little things are to God. "...Well done thou good servant: because thou hast been faithful in a very little, have thou authority over ten cities."

Somewhere I picked up this little saying,
>By a mile, it's a trial.
>By the yard, it's hard.
>But by the inch, it's a cinch.

If you just look at what you want to accomplish or need to sell through the year to earn a living, you may get lost in the big picture, thinking it seems impossible. But when you break it down by what you need to do this month, this week and today, it's much easier. We don't need to worry about the end of the week, the end of the month, or the end of the year—only what we must do today, to be successful. When we do the little things each day, the big things will fall into place. By the inch, it's a cinch. "Success in any line demands a definite aim. He who would achieve true success in life, must keep steadily in view the aim worthy of his endeavors." ED, p. 252.

> **"Success in any line demands a definite aim."—*Education*, p. 252.**

Reading goals are important and illustrate best how much we can accomplish when we apply them. Motivational author Brian Tracy suggests reading a sales book 30 minutes every day. He claims this has totally changed some of his clients from average sales to leaders in sales. Usually leaders are readers. When we read, our vocabulary increases. A study by Georgetown University Medical School reported that in 100 percent of the cases they studied, the IQ increased when the person's vocabulary increased. "God desires man to exercise his reasoning powers; and the study of the Bible will strengthen and elevate the mind as no other study can do." 5T, p. 703.

"Mental culture is what we as a people need...Poverty, humble origin, and unfavorable surroundings need not prevent the cultivation of the mind..." G. W., p. 280.

The Great Controversy, with 678 pages, is an intimidating book to many. But if you set a goal of reading ten pages per day, in only 60 days you will have read it through.

The discipline of goals will go against our feelings. "Always go against your feelings" Arthur Maxwell said at a meeting I attended for literature evangelists. Those words have stuck with me through the years. I was a young worker and he was a great inspiration to me. He shared how some of the greatest victories in his long publishing career (which started with his conversion while canvassing) came when he went against his feelings. Whether he had a cold and was not at 100 percent or just did not want to do a project, he said, "My feeling are almost always wrong, but I always feel good after I have done the right thing." I found that to be true in my own experience. I do not feel like exercising, but after I do I always feel better. I may not feel like getting up and getting started in the morning but I do feel good when I know I have started at the proper time. I do not feel like getting up and being on time for Sabbath School and church, but I feel much better knowing that I set the right example as a church employee and I get the full blessing others have worked hard to prepare. Satan can influence our feelings and make us lazy, but a great way to overcome this is to write out our goals and read them often. Make short and long term goals. Once the objective is clear, it is easier to go against feelings. Good feelings always follow a positive action.

Today I hear people complain because they are gone evenings from their families. But in this work, if we put in our time properly during the week we can have much more time on the weekend than people with less important jobs. God makes this up to us in other ways. When in Africa all my trips away from home were at least a week and sometimes three weeks long. Our children were small. As I left on every trip, I had to fight my feelings. Sometimes as I left I would cry and ask God, am I really doing your will or should I be doing something else where I could be home every night? All of us fight these feelings. So many times I have seen workers take the wider, more traveled road and go to some other "easier work." Usually they have no more time with their families nor do they have the joy that doing this work brings. Even some well meaning church members may encourage this. If you get to feeling this way, go back and read the paragraph, "Comments of Careless Spectators" in *Colporteur Ministry*, p. 14.

My children still recall the good times we had as a family in South Africa. If I was away for very long, we always did something special together when I got back. When our three kids would hear my car pull in, they would all come running out shouting, "Daddy is here! Daddy is here!" and all would start hugging me at the same time. I told my wife many times, "The diamond magnate Harry Oppenheimer is probably the richest man in South Africa, but he cannot buy the joy I feel when I get home." You see the children also took joy in the fact their father was gone working for Jesus. It gave them something special to pray for each evening and morning. In fact, our youngest, who was learning to pray, would pray for me after each blessing for the meal. What does this have to do with goal setting? You see, sometimes my wife's or my vision might get a little foggy, and we had to remind each other of what we were committed to. We believed the Lord called us to Africa, and we had made a commitment of six years to the General Conference. We knew that we were fulfilling a definite need, so with God's help we could be tougher than our circumstances. That does not mean it was easy, nor is it now, but "The success of his[our] labor affords him[us] the purest joy and is the richest recompense for a life of patient toil." CM, p. 14. Our children are grown now, and it is just as hard for me to leave my wife when I go on a trip but our mission and goals help clear our vision.

The balance of family and work has always been a challenge even in Ellen White's day. "It is Satan's regular employment to hinder the work of God...he makes it appear to the mind of the worker that some trifling matter at home is a great importance, and demands his immediate presence. The eye of the worker not being single to the glory of God, he leaves the work unfinished rushes home...stitch after stitch is dropped, never to be taken up again. This pleases the enemy... he gives his hand full of trouble... if possible to keep him away from the work altogether." *Evangelism*, pp. 654, 655.

Reward yourself and your family when you reach a goal. Buy your wife a gift or do something she would like. In Africa, when I got back from a trip I did something special with the kids. When we are home, our family needs to know they are special. When home, I do all I can to lighten my wife's burdens. Goals help us to manage our time at work and home better.

Most people spend more time planning their vacation than their lives. There are some things over which I have no control, such as a committee that involves my work or a division meeting. I have noticed they do not call and ask if this fits my schedule! But there are other meetings and events that I can control and I consider my family's needs. This is true of all of us wherever we work.

With goals we measure where we need to improve. Sales in any line are not consistent every day or every week, but it is the average of the highs and lows that is important. I have had weeks where I had few sales by Thursday at 5:00 p.m. I didn't stop but continued doing the little things I knew it took to be successful. Then, with the Thursday evening and Friday morning sales the Lord blessed with a great week.

I started a new worker going door to door in a Catholic suburb of St. Louis. By Wednesday afternoon when we stopped to eat at 4:30, we had only a few small sales. This new worker began to question his calling. He said, "Bill we have made 27 demonstrations (I always keep a note pad in my pocket so we can measure our demonstrations against sales and make notes of call backs) and you know we haven't sold much. Tomorrow you will be gone and won't be back until Monday. I don't think a person can make a living at this." I assured him he could. I told him, "I don't know why we haven't sold more, but I can assure you that if you do every day what you and I have the past three days, you will be blessed with success." After we ate, we went out to work those golden hours of the evening on some call backs. That evening we sold all five demonstrations. We had a $1000 week. That was a lot of sales in 1972! He went on to work over fifteen years in the literature ministry. What if we had stopped after 27 demonstrations and not found those last five? First, five families would not have the truth in their home. Second, that person would not have gone on to serve the church as literature evangelist and eventually as a leader for more than 15 years.

I heard a story about making calls that has a good point. It seems a large company had a convention in New York City in a great hall. The hall was filled with sales representatives from across the country. The company president called on the leading salesman to come up front and tell what he did to be the best in the country. This leading salesman was a young man who suffered from stage fright. He had never been to such a large city or gathering. The president ask the scared fellow, "Please tell us the secret of your success." The scared young man looked out at the huge auditorium, filled with smoke and so many strange faces. As he started to faint he said softly, "I can't, I can't——" the President said "What did you say?" And as he collapsed, he said, "See the people, see the people." The President of the company said to the large gathering "That's right son, the secret is to see the people, see the people." When in a sales slump, the best way out is to simply "see the people." There is a reason for success and a reason for failure. In this work the biggest reason for failure is simply not seeing enough people.

If you are serious about seeing more good prospects, Brian Tracy's suggestion is to write down 10 or more things you could do to see more good prospects. Some ideas may be far fetched but write them down. Look at these every day for a week. If you can adjust you schedule or find a new idea to just make one or two more calls a day, it will enhance your income and souls reached.

Lois Boyd of Casper, Wyoming, had received a lead card from someone in the city. This is a city of about 50,000 people. The lead card said, "I have the New Testament and now I want the rest of your books." The individual wrote her name, post office box and city. Since it is impossible to sell a post office box, we wanted to talk with this individual personally. We knew from what she wrote on the card that this was a sure sale and someone who loved our books already. Obviously, we were excited. In Wyoming we didn't get many lead cards as the population was small and scattered.

Unfortunately, we could not find the name in the phone book to get the residential address. In fact, we called information and could not find the name listed. We went to the post office, told them that we were religious workers and knew that was an exception but would they please give us the address of the person who received mail at this post office box? We explained our work. The Postmaster was most generous and looked it up. He said, "Unfortunately, I cannot find an address attached to this post office box." We then went to the electric and gas companies. All tried to cooperate, but for some reason, they could not find a street address for this person. By this time, we had used a couple of hours and I was becoming frustrated. I said, "Lois, we've wasted enough time chasing the devil's rabbit. Let's just go down this street, pull into a neighborhood, knock on a few doors, do the thing we know that will help us be successful and leave this card alone." With that, I stuck the card in my pocket. We drove down the nearest street and began knocking on doors. At the very first house, the lady invited us in. As I started the presentation, the lady introduced us to her sister who was visiting in town and lived far out on a ranch in the country. Immediately, the sister's name sounded familiar. I pulled the card from my pocket and asked the lady, "Is this your card?" She said, "Yes, it is." We sold her and her sister each a set of books that morning.

Now God doesn't work a miracle such as this every day. But He gives us enough miracles that we can see His divine providence. You see, that was obviously God's providential leading for us to knock on that door, that day, in a city with ten thousand houses just at the time that the sister was visiting. No one can ever convince me that was just a coincidence. I will always know that was God's providence! But if we had not been out working doing the things that we knew to do, we could not have experienced God providence.

Although I am in an office, I still go out and work by myself and with our literature evangelists as often as possible. I will get dry as the wood in my desk if I do not. All publishing leaders need this to keep their vision clear and confidence in God's call and providence uppermost in their mind. I have been doing this nearly three decades, and I am recharged every time I sell a book. It has proven to me that this work is effective on any continent and is divinely given to this church. To me, every time that I sell a *Great Controversy*, or the *Conflict of the Ages* set to a family, or even the *Bible Story*, (which is a mini *Conflict of the Ages* series including the *Great Controversy* story) it is a miracle. After each sale that I make, I walk out of the home saying, "Thank you Lord. Thank you for your divine leading in this home. Thank you for allowing me to be Your messenger, Your man in this hour." Even after all these years and having seen it so many times, it is still a miracle to me when I see Catholics, Baptists, and non-believers purchase our books and love them. When we get letters in our office from people telling us how these books have changed their lives and have drawn them to the Bible, I know that it is God providence. We experience this only as we do the Lord's work.

In following our goals, we must always keep our eyes open for those individuals whom Providence has led us to. We will meet people who are ready to be brought into the church now. Our work is mostly a seed-sowing work, but there are many who are to be reaped now. The closer we get to the end of time, the more we will see of this. Elder Ted Smith, Associate Publishing Director in the Southern Union, told me the following story which I believe emphasizes the point that we must be continually watching for God's providence and going the extra mile for those who are on the verge of the kingdom.

"Early in 1952, shortly after I began my literature ministry. I was working in a rural county in Tennessee. On that cold, January evening, the clouds were ominous. As a cold drizzle began to fall, I was hastening from one country home to another trying to reach my goal for the day. I could see people scurrying trying to get home before the weather got too bad. The radio in my car was blasting the bad weather report that a terrible snow storm was imminent.

"One lady told me I had better get home before dark because I might get stranded on the road. Since I was about 25 miles from home, her advice was well founded. But I still hadn't reached my goal for the day. So I decided to see two more homes. After leaving the first home, the weather had really gotten bad so I decided to start for home. The snow had already covered the ground. The country road was narrow. I was praying I wouldn't meet another car before I got to the main highway.

"As I began to descend the hill down to the highway, there was a house sitting below the level of the road down an embankment. You could only see the top of the house from the road. A voice spoke inside me saying to stop at this house. Another voice said to go home. But still, some voice kept saying to stop, stop! I slowed down to look at the house. I decided that no one lived there because I didn't see smoke coming from the chimney. I pushed my Pontiac up into second gear and proceeded down the slope to the main highway. But a little voice inside me kept saying, you should have stopped! You should have stopped!

"The highway had only a few cars on the road. I thought about my wife and little son at home. I knew she would be worried about me, but there were no telephones to call. I kept prodding my way up that snow dusty road while the car radio was blasting the terrible news of impending catastrophic weather, warning everyone to get off the road. Here and there, I could see cars off the side of the road. I kept inching along while the voice inside me kept saying, "You should have stopped!"

"I arrived home to see my wife anxiously peering out of the ice capped window nervously looking for my car. We prayed and thanked God for my safe arrival. Our usual conversation was about how our day had gone. I would give her reports about the people I met, my successes and failures. I told her about the house I was so impressed to stop at but didn't and how troubled I was because I didn't. She tried to reassure me that I did the right thing because I could go back another day. Besides, I wasn't sure if anyone lived there. That night was a restless night for me. There were no televisions, at least not very many in those days, so we had to depend on the radio for news. The radio by my bed was giving the weather news continuously. All that night I was troubled in my spirit. I could hear the cracking of tree limbs in my back yard. Looking out of the window, the power lines were sagging as they got larger in diameter from the accumulation of snow and ice. I prayed to God that our lights wouldn't go out.

"I got up early next morning, as was my custom, still troubled, troubled in my spirit, I got on my knees and prayed to God. "Dear Lord," I said, "Why am I so troubled about that house? Show me Lord, please show me." A little voice inside me said you've got to go back. You've got to go back. I put on my high top boots, went out to my car to remove two feet of snow off it and started the engine so it would warm up. By the time I got back into the house, my wife had awakened and asked me what I was fixing to do. I told her I was going back to that house I missed. She began to cry and plead, "Honey, please don't go. It is too bad out there. You can go when the weather gets better. Don't you see there's no one on the street?" I told her, "Hon, I've got to go. I prayed about it, and I'm impressed to go." She knew I was determined to go. I was a good driver because I had learned at an early age by driving tractors and trucks and all types of vehicles on the farm through snow and ice across the fields and ditches. So the confidence she had in me as a good driver was reassuring. But in this weather there wouldn't be anyone out there to help if I got into trouble. We prayed and I headed my car down the street slowly out of my neighborhood to the main street. There was no one on the street but me. I began to question my sanity. A little voice began to whisper in my ear saying, "Go back, go back." But I could still hear that small voice saying, "You've got to go on." The road was slick and icy, trees had fallen, cars were side ways and abandoned. Some were in ditches, some stranded in the middle of the road, but I kept moving slowly toward my destination.

"As I neared the little road where I was to turn off the highway, the entrance was indistinguishable. I didn't know if I was going off in a ditch or whether I was going in the road. I paused to whisper a prayer, "God, please don't let me miss the road and drive into the ditch." I started to move on but my car just sat there and spun it wheels. I got out and let some air out of my

tires—an old trick I learned as a boy on the farm. I got back into
my car and rocked it shifting from reverse to low gear a few times.
It started moving in the direction I hoped would be the road. The
Lord had answered my prayer. Slowly, I crept up the hill with my
car in second gear and arrived at the top of the hill. I stopped my
car in the middle of the road. Surely no one would be as foolish as
I was to get out in this bad weather so I was sure no one else
would come by. Before I got out of the car, I whispered a little
prayer of thanks to God and started sliding down the slope to the
house. I banged on the door and by the sound, I could tell that the
house was empty. I peered through the dirty window and my sus-
picion was confirmed because on the floor was nothing but rub-
bish and trash. A little voice inside me began to ridicule me telling me how foolish I was to come out in this bad weather to an
empty house.

"I said to God, 'God, why did you put such a burden on my
heart to come out here if the house was empty?' I began to feel
frustrated and angry but that still small voice said to go around
to the back. I slid down the hill to the side of the house and there
was a door. I banged on the door and I heard the same empty
sound coming from within. I began to feel foolish but something
said to keep knocking. After a few minutes, the door slowly opened
and there stood a little girl in her early teens. Her teeth were
clattering from the cold. Her hair was disheveled, and I asked if
her parents were home. She said, "Yes," and invited me in. The
house was cold and icy. There was a mother and eight children in
that house. No lights, no heat, no nothing, and very little furni-
ture! It was so dark in the house I could hardly see. I went back
to my car and got a flash light. What I saw was sad. I asked if
they had a lamp? The answer was yes, but they had no oil.

"I went back to my car and backed it down the hill to the highway. A short distance down the road was a country general store.
In those days, general stores sold everything. Usually the store
was out front and the owner lived in a house a few yards in the
back. I waded in waist-deep snow to the house and started banging on the door. I knew the people would probably be upset over
being disturbed, but I had to do it. After a while, a gentleman
came to the door. He did look a little upset, but he was nice and
very polite to me. I introduced myself as Pastor Smith on a mission of mercy who had traveled 25 miles to help a family in dire
need. I told him the problem and what I wanted from him. He

invited me into his warm house while he got ready to let me into the store. On the way out to the store, I told him I only had twenty dollars. Twenty dollars would buy a lot in those days. We went in, and I bought bread, bologna, beans, peaches and anything that could be prepared quickly. I also bought oil for the lamp, as much coal and kindling for the stove as I could get in my car. While I was getting the supplies the gentleman said to me, 'Rev, if you get more than the twenty dollars worth, you can pay me later.' I went back to the house and made a fire and helped to prepare food for the family.

"I arrived back home to my waiting wife and told her of how God had directed me to that family. We both got on our knees and praised God for His leading in our lives and directing me to this family in need.

"The church got involved and I would drive out every Sabbath morning and bring these people to church. Soon that mother and all eight children were baptized into the Seventh-day Adventist Church. But the story doesn't end here. Out of that family came three teachers, one minister, two engineers, one chaplain in the army, and one nurse! Praise God for His leading in our lives. Who knows what will result if we follow God's leading!"

Set well thought-out goals that are realistic, but that will push you to new growth. When you reach these goals, set bigger ones. Have a definite work plan, but allow for the door of providence when it opens. It is an exciting and fun door. I can assure you in this work it will open.

Chapter 11

"Look among the nations and watch — be utterly astounded! For I will work a work in your days which you would not believe, though it were told you."
Habakkuk 1:5 NKJV

Why Publish?

Why publish? Or more specifically, why have a direct sales force (literature evangelism) in this age of technology and information? Isn't direct sales passe? Many church members and administrators ask this question today. I'd would like to answer these questions briefly in the following six points:

1. God Ordained The Literature Ministry And Said It Would Continue Until Probation Closes.

"God has ordained the canvassing work." 6T, p. 313. "The canvassing work, properly conducted is missionary work of the highest order." Ibid. "As long as probation continues, there will be opportunity for the canvasser to work . . . Until in heaven is spoken the word, 'It is finished,' there will always be places for labor, and hearts to receive the message." 6T, p. 478

2. The Printed Word Is The Most Permanent Form Of Witness.

When the Lord inspired these words written above in the first paragraph, He knew of satellites in the sky, E-Mail, fax machines, and all of the marvelous inventions of communication that we have today. The purpose of all knowledge that He has given man is for His glory and the hastening of His coming. God will use all of these means, but the one invention that is still the most permanent and lasting is the printed word.

I remember when transistors came out and everybody had to have a transistor radio. They were small and inexpensive and could be carried everywhere. It was claimed then that it would be the end of the print media. Well there are still places where not everybody has a radio, and in homes with all the most modern gadgets, people are still buying printed material, and it is a booming business. In every developing country, people who cannot read understand the importance of learning to read and will sacrifice much for the privilege. Reading is the most basic of education. When the electricity goes out, people can still read. People in developed countries may say the electricity will always be available here. We live in an age of urban terrorism when 16 year old computer hackers have been able to penetrate the Pentagon information system. One knowledgeable person with a small computer can crash a city power system. There are other challenges to western cities too numerous to state here that will cause the fulfillment of the prophecy, "The time will come when these books will be sought for and read." CM, p. 150. A reading church member is usually a stronger church member.

Talk about the permanent printed page. A *Great Controversy* sold many decades ago by a literature evangelist, was given to Dr. Raymond Browning in Greenwood, Mississippi. He was told that this book had a lot of history and he might enjoy it. It seems that this individual who had the book didn't really want it. The doctor did. He read it and came under conviction. He found the Voice of Prophecy radio program which also taught the Sabbath truth and started the Bible correspondence course. Today he is a very active Seventh-day Adventist Church member. How many others did this book influence through the decades? We do not know. But this story could be told over and over across the world.

I worked with some of the missionaries who were part of the great Kasai project. They shared this story with me and part of it is told in the October 19, 1972 *Review and Herald*. Kasai providence is a huge area bigger than the state of Texas in the country then known as Zaire. The president of the country became concerned because of some the growing national churches which could be a political spring board for rival politicians. He outlawed many of these churches and recognized only a handful of religious organizations he trusted. By God's providence and some good church leadership our church was named among the few that people could belong to. The government also published what each group believed.

The first 12 years of a mission there, we had only 150 converts. Political problems caused the missionary stationed there to have to leave. Then for another 11 years there was little growth. Then these laws were passed.

Many years before someone had sold a French *Great Controversy,* and it eventually came into the hands of one of the leaders of an African church. He read and taught it but did not know there was a church that kept the Sabbath until the laws were passed that caused him to search. One day he found our mission and asked if he could join our church. "Well of course," was the response of our small mission representing less than 300 members. He then asked if his church could join our church. "Well of course," was the response. "And how many members do you have?" The answer must have sounded too incredible to be believed for this struggling mission. The answer was 50,000! Another large group came whose leader had studied the Voice of Prophecy Bible course. Where he got the Bible course is not known, but in Africa, like most places, most Bible course enrollment come from literature evangelists. Much of the millennium will be needed to share our salvation stories! All these searching people had to have studies. It was a long process and administrative challenge, but that area is now one of our church's biggest unions.

But could this happen in your city or country? Could sudden changes come to your community that would cause people to search the Scriptures. Of course! Recently one satellite tilted for a still unknown reason, and suddenly thousands of cell phones and beepers in the U. S. were out for days, including those of many doctors and hospitals. Could this be a fore warning of our dependence on electronic gadgets? How many people will you leave the permanent and powerful printed page with while you have time?

3. A Book Is Organized.

A book says the same thing over and over each time we pick it up, and it doesn't argue back. When we give our testimony, sometimes we may feel indifferent. We may have a cold or be tired. We may not be as patient as we should be, but the book is always the same. Recently, a Church of Christ minister called the Kentucky-Tennessee Conference office and asked to see the one responsible for selling our literature. He was referred to the Publishing Director, David Haugsted. David was surprised to meet an elderly pastor who had spent his whole life in the ministry of another church. He was on the staff of one of the largest churches of that denomination. He told David the following story:

It seems the pastor had sent in a lead card asking for information on health books. When the literature evangelist arrived, the pastor was not interested at that time and did not purchase. He did not tell the literature evangelist that he was a minister. But he did tell him that he wasn't feeling well. The literature evangelist asked if he could pray for him, and the pastor agreed. As our worker left he gave the minister the *Great Controversy*. The minister laid the book aside. When he did look at it, he knew it was published by Seventh-day Adventists and planned to throw it away. But for some reason, he just laid it aside and almost forgot it. His illness got worse. One day while lying in bed, he picked it up to see what it said. He read the book through and came under the conviction that its message was right. He studied it more, then he came to see David. He said, "You know, I would like to sell these." He also told David, "You know, for many years I've argued with the Seventh-day Adventists, but I can see now that you are right." David asked him, "What makes the difference now?" The minister said, "This book never argued back, and it always said the same thing."

4. There Is Recreative Power In God's Word.

"For the word of God is living and powerful and sharper than a two-edged sword. Hebrews 4:12. I love the way Ellen White states it in the book *Education*, p. 126. "The creative power that called the worlds into existence is in the word of God." What a powerful thought! When we handle God's word, we handle the same creative power that called the worlds into existence. That makes the literature ministry a very important work. Our books change people's lives, both young and old.

> **"The creative power that called the worlds into existence is in the word of God."—*Education*, p. 126.**

After we served three years in Africa, we returned on furlough to Wichita, Kansas, where we joined the local church and began the literature ministry. It had been approximately eight years since I had sold any books in that area. One day a friend of ours invited us out to eat. As we sat down in the restaurant, I noticed a lady and her husband sitting across the room having dinner. I told my wife, "Honey, I know I sold that woman books." My wife replied, "Bill, it's been years since you've sold books here. You do not know her." I said, "Yes, I remember her. She wore leg braces, and I remember her face. I know that I sold her books. I want to go over and ask if she is enjoying them." My wife pleaded with me again. "Bill, please don't embarrass me. You do not know that lady. We haven't been here for years." "But Honey," I persisted, "I'm sure that I sold her books." Well, I went over and asked her if she remembered me. I told her that I was sure I had sold her two sets of books, the *Bible Story* with a large book and later the *Bedtime Story* with another large book. She responded, "Yes you did." I said, "I remember you had a little boy who loved those books." She said, "Yes I did and he did love those books and did come to know the Lord through them. He was playing near the street and was killed a couple of years ago when a car hit him." I expressed my sympathy and reassured her of the hope of Christ's second coming. Because of that mother's love and the wonderful tools that were left in her home, I have the hope I will see that little boy in the earth made new.

Recently, I met the Spearn family in Melbourne, Florida. Both Mr. and Mrs. Spearn were aeronautical engineers who worked for the NASA space program. Literature evangelists Rick Matthaeus and Joe Holloway called at their home. Mr. Spearn purchased almost all of our books for his family. He had two small children, and he and his wife were concerned about teaching them moral values they thought were needed although they were not active members of any church at the time. Mr. Spearn's job was to meet the astronauts when they returned on the space shuttle and debrief them. Sometimes they would be on the eastern side of the United States and other times on the western side of the country, depending on where NASA planned to land the space shuttle. This depended on the weather.

While waiting for the astronauts to come down, Mr. Spearn often had to wait, sometimes for days. He had plenty of time to read. He took with him two books, *The Desire of Ages* and the

Great Controversy. He read these books, and they brought conviction to his heart. He took the *Great Controversy* back to his wife and asked her to read it and let him know what she thought of this book. She went to the library, checked out all of the historical quotes and found the book to be correct. They read about the Sabbath and believed it should be observed, and one day they just walked into our church in Melbourne, Florida, never having had a Bible study. They have been active members every since. In fact, now they both lead out in many activities.

Mrs. Spearn made a statement that emphasizes a point about the recreative power in these books. She said, "Since my youth, I've always believed in evolution. All the schools that I attended taught it, and I've never questioned it. But as I read these books, everything else made so much sense, I knew that this had to be true too." You see, even the most educated and the most trained minds, when they read the Bible and our books with an open mind, will be transformed. There's a need for those who have advanced degrees in biology and the various sciences to develop arguments against evolution. But in the end it has to be the Holy Spirit speaking to one's heart, and the most powerful testimony is not man's argument but God's Word.

5. Literature Evangelism Develops A Christian Experience.

"God hath dealt to each man a measure of faith." Romans 12:3. God has wired the human mind to worship and serve Him. Humanity has perverted this in all kinds of ways. But if we really get to know God, it has to be by experience. As we walk with Him through highs and lows, and we see His unconditional love and His providence in our lives, we really get to know Him. It makes our prayer life more real and Bible study more vibrant. I have seen many individuals through the years who come into the literature ministry and develop into dynamic and powerful witnesses for the Lord. I've seen many who were very shy in the beginning, become bold in the Lord as they continue praying and working, asking for God's blessings. *Colporteur Ministry* tells us that this the very best training for ministers. Our Union president, Elder Malcolm Gordon, told me, "Bill I got my Master of Divinity degree, but the six summers that I spent canvassing did more for my ministry that any course that I took in college." Space does not allow me to share with you the many, many stories of individuals I have witnessed whose lives have been changed because of their dedicated service in literature ministry.

"In the common walks of life there is many a man patiently treading the round of daily toil, unconscious that he posses powers which, if called into action, would raise him to an equality with the world's most honored men." DA, p. 250.

6. People Need People.

There is a song by this title, and it is so true. Our church is involved in some exciting evangelism with the latest satellite technology, as we should be. We have down links and up links, but all of these are worthless without the vital human link. God has given us this high tech for one purpose—His glory. The book *Mega Trends 2000* warns of the need in our ever increasing high tech society that humanity should be careful not to lose our high touch.

The human link is still the most important. It is the human link to whom we talk, not a computer. It is human link who knocks on a door and invites people to come to our meetings. It is still the human link who prays in a home. It is the human link who invites people home to eat, shakes a hand, embraces another, laughs when we laugh, cries when we cry. It is the human link who prays for love ones and friends.

Is literature evangelism/colporteur ministry outmoded, passe? Only if we lose our first love, our vision, and forget divine counsel. God uses people, and people need people. The literature evangelists of this church still knock on more doors and visit more nonmembers than any department in the church.

*"Write the vision and make it plain on tablets.
That he may run who reads it. For the vision is yet
for an appointed time; but at the end it will speak,
and it will not lie. Though it tarries , wait for it;
Because it will surely come, it will not tarry."*
Habakkuk 2:2, 3

Conclusion

Throughout my years in the literature ministry, I've used Isaiah 55:11—"My word shall not returned to me void" on letterheads and newsletters. It has been my promise and great encouragement. You could call it my theme. I know God will honor His promise. In fact He says, "God is not a man, that He should lie; neither the Son of Man, that He should repent; hath He said, and shall He not do it? Or hath He spoken, and shall He not make it good?" Numbers 23:19. We are all excited from the first fruits we see by our labor, but there is an exciting harvest coming from all of the seeds that we've sown. There is going to be something beyond our comprehension, "Now we see in a mirror dimly..." 2 Cor. 13:12, NIV. Here are just a couple of mind stretching promises. "It is true that some buy the books and lay them on the shelf. . . . The time will come when these books will be sought for and read." 6T, p. 313. "More than a thousand will be converted in one day, most of whom will trace their first conviction to the reading of our publications." *Review and Herald*, November 10, 1885. "For our light and momentary troubles are achieving for us an eternal glory that far out weighs them all. So we fix our eyes not on what is seen, but on what is unseen. For what is seen is temporary, but what is unseen is eternal." 2 Cor. 4:17, 18. What re-

127

joicing there is going to be in the earth made new when the literature evangelists meet those people, those thousands of people to
whom they sold and gave literature. I believe it will be said of
them as it was of David, "They served God's purpose in their generation."